beyond
postmodern
politics

Honi Fern Haber

beyond
postmodern
politics

Lyotard

Rorty

Foucault

ROUTLEDGE New York • London

Published in 1994 by

Routledge
29 West 35 Street
New York, NY 10001

Published in Great Britain by

Routledge
11 New Fetter Lane
London EC4P 4EE

Library of Congress Cataloging in Publication Data

Haber, Honi Fern, 1958–
    Beyond postmodern politics : Lyotard, Rorty, Foucault / Honi Fern
Haber.
        p. cm.
    Includes bibliographical references (p. 149) and index.
    ISBN 0-415-90822-1   ISBN 0-415-90823-X
    1. Individualism.   2. Community.   3. Difference (Philosophy)—
Political aspects.   4. Opposition (Political science)
5. Postmodernism—Political aspects.   6. Lyotard, Jean François.
7. Rorty, Richard.   8. Foucault, Michel.   I. Title.   II. Title:
Beyond post-modern politics.
JC571.H1714   1994
320′.01—dc20   93-48108
                                                                    CIP

British Library Cataloguing information also available.

Contents

Acknowledgments

This book could not have been completed without the assistance and support of a number of people. I am glad to have a chance to acknowledge at least some of them here.

I would like first of all to acknowledge the help of Joseph Margolis, Richard Shusterman, Alexander Nehamas, and Jitendra Mohanty. Their comments and criticisms were of great help to the improvements of early drafts of this book. I wish especially to acknowledge my gratitude to Joseph Margolis, not just for his comments and criticisms, but also for his emotional support and unfailing good humor; he is responsible for keeping my head above water. I wish too to thank my editor Maureen MacGrogan for believing in this project and for all her help in getting it to press.

I also wish to acknowledge the debt this project owes to a community of friends and scholars who have been patient, supportive, and inspirational. In this context I would like to single out Gregg Horowitz and Michael Meyer, who have patiently listened to, and helped me refine, my thoughts. Sandra Bartky, Ann Ferguson, and Jana Sawicki have each in their own way helped me to believe that I too could be taken seriously as a philosopher. Their unaffected and warmhearted generosity is indeed an inspiration; I hope I can be as encouraging to others as they have been to me. Above all, I would like to thank Roger J. H. King who has been my harshest critic and greatest support; without him this project could never have been completed.

Finally, I wish to thank my family: my parents Millicent and Charles Haber, whose confidence and support have been unfailing; my brother Lloyd Haber, who is proud to tell his friends that what his sister does is "think"; and my grandparents Elsa and Saul Kalin, to whom I dedicate this work—they would have been so proud.

Introduction

There is no view from nowhere. We can never leave all our prejudices behind and operate from a wholly disinterested standpoint, but our prejudices become dangerous only when they are dogmatic, kept hidden from view and not open to discussion. This being the case, I would like at the outset to make clear, albeit in a preliminary way, the political and philosophical commitments which inform this project.

The work presented here is part of an ongoing project to formulate an oppositional politics where politics is conceived broadly enough to include what bourgeois liberalism has either relegated to the sphere of the private, or suppressed altogether. Bourgeois liberalism is part of a philosophical tradition which views individuals as essentially autonomous, self-interested, and appetitive, and which masks its interested values as being the objective and universal values of science and rationality.[1] This metaphysical and ontological background leads bourgeois liberalism to value possessive individualism above all else,[2] and is used to justify the dominance of white, patriarchal, classist, and racist regimes.

I differ from this tradition on many points. I hold with the poststructuralist insight that the notion of the individual is correlative with the notion of the subject, and that since subjects are inscribed in language they are always cultural, historical, and social entities. This notion of the subject gives a place of privilege to community, for our interests are always the interests of some community or another.

I also differ from the liberal tradition in believing that there is no universal community of rational beings. Each one of us is a member of many different communities, and these different communities do not form a coherent, or unified in the sense of essential or unchanging, whole. Given this standpoint, I will argue that any viable political theory must be able to accommodate the view that a subject is never singular or autonomous, but always exists as a member of some com-

1

munity; a subject is always, as I shall put it, a "subject-in-community." As will become clear in the final two chapters, this term is central to my theory of empowerment.

The term *subject-in-community* is not meant to denote a static entity. Since the self is a member of many different communities and so is essentially plural, it is also always capable of being redescribed. Because each subject is always plural in this way it is made up of multiple selves, and so any community can always be deconstructed to reveal plural and possibly conflicting interests. This is why I will argue that politics is always potentially, and even inherently, oppositional. There will always be voices excluded, repressed, or suppressed by any particular community formation. This conclusion is not, however, negative; in fact, I will argue in the final chapter that this ever-present possibility of the other (whether in actual others or in ourselves) guarantees the possibility of a rich understanding of ourselves and our relation to others, and also points at a mechanism that explains why it is possible to resist hegemonic power regimes.

My notion of oppositional politics understands a political theory to be viable to the extent to which it is able to construct itself to pay attention to difference—to those voices or concerns that have been marginalized by disciplinary and normalizing power regimes. The broader the political sphere the more possibilities exist to give voice to those who have been marginalized or silenced, and it is with the voicing of marginalized groups that my notion of oppositional politics is primarily concerned.

Where classical liberalism defends itself by positing ahistorical foundations and legitimations, I claim that economics, religion, science, and culture are all formed against the background of the political. By this I mean that they are always the result of a creative enterprise, an enterprise whose possibility for new creations is always open. But this cannot be understood as resulting from a private exchange between the idiosyncratic artist and her or his muse (this will be taken up again in my criticism of Rorty's Romantic notion of the artist); rather creation is only possible given the tools of our vocabulary, and since vocabularies are always already social, cultural, and historical products, they always speak for an interested viewpoint—though we may not always be conscious of this interested dimension. It is from this standpoint that I argue that vocabularies mirror political perspectives.

My overall project, one to which I hope this work contributes, attempts to create a space for oppositional politics that can also be described as a "politics of difference" (though as will become clear in the final chapter, my use of a "politics of difference" differs in some important respects from current usage). The present work aids this project in both criticizing and combining certain insights of poststructuralism with certain insights of postmodernism. I use poststructuralism and postmodernism to provide oppositional struggles with a framework for the formation of a viable political model: a politics of difference. This is my bias, my interested political program. However, while the insights and sympathies of poststructuralism and postmodernism are useful, the question which motivates the present project is whether the politicizing of poststructuralism and postmodernism as put forth by its leading spokesmen—and in the following chapters I have chosen to discuss Lyotard, Rorty, and Foucault—can actually give us a viable political theory. It can be used, but can it be adopted? Can there be a postmodern politics? In fact, I shall argue that there cannot.

This project, then, does three things. First, it explores both what is useful and what is harmful in the postmodernism of Lyotard and Rorty, and the poststructuralism of Foucault, for the project of an oppositional politics, and then suggests ways to move beyond postmodern politics to a politics of difference. Second, my thesis calls into question the very notion of a postmodern politics and any politics of difference which accepts the law of difference as an absolute. A careful analysis of poststructuralism and postmodernism for oppositional politics is necessary even for those of us who are sympathetic to the postmodern project, because the idea of a postmodern politics is becoming a fad without its having been subject to enough careful political scrutiny, and a careful examination of postmodern politics will show it to be in fact harmful to oppositional politics. While what postmodern politics speaks to is not a fad, since it speaks to the needs of the marginalized Other—to women, to people of color, to gays and lesbians, to the working class, to the poor and homeless . . . and while poststructuralism and postmodernism are useful insofar as they bring such needs into the forefront of contemporary political debate, I will finally argue that it, perhaps ironically, denies those needs any political voice. In insisting on the universalization of difference, postmodern politics forecloses on the possibility of community and subjects necessary to oppositional resistance.

The terms *postmodernism* and *poststructuralism* are often confused and confusing terms. So even though the terms and their relationship to each other will be expanded in the following chapters, it might be helpful for me to outline the use I will make of such concepts, both what I borrow and what I criticize.

The main feature of postmodern politics that concerns me here is the eschewal of what Lyotard calls "grand narratives"—anything that indicates essences beyond the context of a particular language game. This means, for example, that there can be no absolute ideal Human Essence, or Rationality, or Morality. The postmodern borrows from the Saussurean/Derridian strain of structuralism/poststructuralism the notion of difference and play as well as a version of Nietzschean perspectivism: everything we are and do is formulated within language (a formulation which, as Lacan aptly notes, we do not have total conscious control over), where language is understood as an open-ended sign system. Our possibilities are as infinite and as open to redescription as are the opportunities for redescription given to us by language.

Since the self is then a "narrative construction," and language a potentially infinite system of signs, the self can always be redescribed, given an alternative perspective. I would, however, reject those who conclude from this Nietzschean perspectivism that there is no subject (no author). I maintain that all the poststructuralist thesis necessitates—and I do not mean that this "all" is not radical from the standpoint of the tradition of subjectivity inherited from Descartes and Kant—is the claim that the self need not be a consistent, unchanging, or even coherent entity. "Changing one's mind" is not the domain of the feminine, rather it demarcates the nature of the poststructurally concerned linguistic self.

I borrow from poststructuralism for my requirements of a "viable" politics: a viable politics is one which can accommodate difference. If the self is formed within the confines of language, then it is always and necessarily a social construct. If poststructuralism owes a debt to Nietzsche, it also owes a debt to Wittgenstein; there are no private languages. But then, though caprice may be an inherent feature of the Nietzschean subject, play (self-description) is limited to the possible combinations of a social vocabulary that is always the vocabulary of some community or another. We always find ourselves a member of some community though we are all many "selves" and members of many "communities."

A politics like my own, which wishes to retain some of the insights of poststructuralism, must find a notion of solidarity which does not universalize totality. Such a universalizing of totality would amount to ignoring the plural, or "protean," nature of selves, community, and culture. But our interests are neither static, nor are they necessarily common. Poststructuralism and postmodern politics is useful for arguing against the validity of the universalizing of totality. But I also claim, and this will become an important part of my critical analysis of poststructuralism and postmodernism, that just as we must not universalize totality, so too must we avoid universalizing difference. Such a universalization would amount to denying the possibility of any and all structure, and, I will argue, such a position is incoherent. We cannot think or speak, much less act, in any purposeful manner without having structured our world and our interests in some heuristically useful way. Without some notion of structure (unity) and some allowance for a legitimate recognition of similarities between ourselves and others, there can be no subject, community, language, or culture. My thesis argues that because poststructuralism universalizes difference, it cannot give us a useful political theory. I will show that it is just this tendency to universalize difference which argues for the rejection of Lyotard, Rorty, and even Foucault as contenders for theorists of oppositional politics. In repudiating the universalizing of difference, I also wish to revitalize the importance of solidarity. I will argue in the final chapter that our identities are formed within communities of similar interests. Those interests can be positive or negative, and when they are negative, they can act as catalysts of change.

We can take power only by recognizing it, and an important component of our ability to recognize what has been suppressed or distorted is recognizing our similarity with others—recognizing that we are part of yet another community. Such recognition unmasks the political nature of what has been understood as a "purely private" phenomenon. Making the private public, and hence amenable to political debate, is a necessary step in empowerment. I argue that recognizing that the points at which our "deviant" behaviors are shared with or similar to others' and are not the result of some monstrous, idiosyncratic aberration, enables the politicizing of "marginalized voices." This is how sexuality, for example, or eating disorders, or certain forms of "insanity" become empowered and politicized. My critique of postmodern politics centers then on my rejection of its disjunction: *either* totality *or* difference; each member of this team will have to be reconceptualized to accommodate their synthesis.

Although I argue that Lyotard, Rorty, and Foucault are unsuccessful in their respective attempts at postmodern and poststructuralist politics, I am not interested merely in critiquing individual theorists. Rather I am interested in examining the repercussions of the major themes of poststructuralism and postmodernism for an oppositional political theory. Those particular poststructuralists and postmodernists I critique are meant to serve as exemplars of the more general problems I shall address in my analysis. My discussion will focus on what I take to be a representative sample of those philosophers at the forefront of the "postmodern debate." Here I would like again to acknowledge that the terms *postmodern* and *poststructuralist* are confusing even within the literature. They are sometimes used as if they are interchangeable, and in fact, in the secondary literature they are often used with capricious abandon. I think the confusion between them arises in part because postmodernism presupposes poststructuralist analysis and especially its view of the subject as a linguistic entity, and because the politicizing of poststructuralism overlaps the concerns of postmodern politics.

I will be returning to and elaborating on these two terms within the course of this work. I ask the reader to be patient. For the moment let me say that I understand Lyotard, Rorty, and Foucault all to be inheritors of the poststructuralist position even if they are not themselves avowedly poststructuralist. Rorty's poststructuralism is only implicit, while Lyotard is a poststructuralist who is also a postmodernist. By that I mean he is concerned with the Other, which along with an understanding of language as a differential sign system, is the hallmark of poststructuralism. Lyotard is also concerned, as is Rorty, with the postmodern repudiation of all grand narratives. And here it might help to clarify terms if I quote Lyotard:

> . . . to the extent that science does not restrict itself to stating useful regularities and seeks the truth, it is obliged to legitimate the rules of its own game. It then produces a discourse of legitimation with respect to its own status, a discourse called philosophy. I will use the term *modern* to designate any science that legitimates itself with reference to a metadiscourse of this kind making an explicit appeal to some grand narrative, such as the dialectics of Spirit, the hermeneutics of meaning, the emancipation of the rational or working subject, of the creation of wealth. . . . Simplifying to the extreme, I define *postmodern* as incredulity toward metanarratives.[3]

The repudiation of all grand narratives is the mark of the postmodern, though such repudiation is only explainable with reference to poststructuralism and its thesis of difference. This is why I argue that postmodernism is correlative to poststructuralism.

Foucault is explicitly poststructuralist, though he is not, at least explicitly, postmodernist. He does not think we can operate without grand narratives or legitimating discourses. This is our fate as linguistic and hence cultural subjects. What he teaches us is that even if we refuse to be postmodernists, we can nevertheless remain skeptical about our use of legitimating discourse. Subjects are always caught within the matrices of power regimes. Such power regimes are always open to being deconstructed. This means that while we must operate with legitimizing discourses, we can also acknowledge that such discourses are always subject to delegitimation. It is this flexibility which makes Foucault's theory more useful for the purposes of oppositional politics than either Lyotard's or Rorty's.

In the following pages I examine the poststructuralist and postmodern themes of Lyotard, Rorty, and Foucault, to assess their usefulness for oppositional politics. I have chosen to discuss Rorty because he is the most influential representative of the Anglo-American branch of postmodern politics. Of the influential European proponents, I have chosen to concentrate my analysis on Lyotard and Foucault. I have chosen Lyotard not only because in making the term *postmodern* familiar to many philosophic audiences he is an obvious choice, but also because he most directly enters into debate with Rorty over how postmodern politics ought to be expressed. There is a progression from one to the other which makes my choice of representatives heuristically useful; the move from Lyotard to Rorty reveals for us progressive attempts to solve the problems engendered for political theory by the postmodern commitment to a radical pluralism ("paganism" in Lyotard's terms, "ironism" in Rorty's). Furthermore, the fact that Lyotard, Rorty, and Foucault are explicit about their political commitments makes them natural candidates for my project in a way that other exponents of the postmodern position, such as Derrida, are not.

My exposition then will proceed as follows. I discuss Lyotard first because in my view he represents the least successful attempt at pluralist politics ("pluralist politics" is being used here to denote a politics which accommodates the demands of difference and so is a necessary component of oppositional politics). His "paganism" gives way to Kantianism because he remains stuck within the old framework. He sees his paganism as resulting in relativism and feels this relativism must be overcome because he retains an enlightenment conception of politics.

Rorty is an advance over Lyotard if only because he recognizes that the problem of relativism belongs to a paradigm inconsistent with the commitments of the postmodern thesis. However, Rorty also believes that ironism engenders certain difficulties: most notably he is concerned to save certain liberal humanist values. His attempt at reconciling ironism or pluralism with liberalism leads him into deep inconsistencies, the most unfortunate of which is his rejuvenation of the public/

private distinction. This distinction does violence to all that is visionary in pluralist politics. Rorty represents what Michael Walzer has called "American pluralism." His analysis disperses power to individuals and groups but is then recentralized; power is regathered at the focal point of "we liberals," a category that is merely a substitute for the traditional locus of sovereignty. He is thus unable to remain true to the radical pluralism demanded by his postmodern commitments.

Unlike Rorty, Foucault does not stabilize (or authorize) a locus of power. His thesis is rather that "power is exercised from innumerable points."[4] Instead of a focal point of sovereignty, he postulates an endless network of power relations. Thus Foucault can be commended as insisting—as Rorty does not—on the ubiquitous nature of power (and hence of politics). Such a thesis abolishes the viability of distinguishing between the private and the public. It recognizes that childbearing, household concerns, sex, desires, needs, fashion, education—in short, all things traditionally understood as belonging to the realm of the private—have important political dimensions, since their genealogy is rooted in networks of power. For this reason Foucault's analysis of politics is most frequently adopted as a methodological tool for oppositional politics and as such is seminal to my investigation into the viability of such a politics. Furthermore, the thesis of the ubiquitous nature of power must be the end result of any consistent postmodern or poststructuralist politics and, I will argue, that part of it which must be saved whatever else may turn out to be untenable in the postmodern or poststructuralist position.[5]

In this introduction I have touched upon the main themes which will be developed in the following discussion. I do not expect that it is yet convincing, or even that it is necessarily clear. My hope is that it will be more convincing by the time the reader has come to the last page. And if by the last page there are still things that remain unclear or unconvincing, this too is to be expected, and not only because we may have different, and not necessarily compatible interests, for the task of speaking is an infinite labor. I hope that at the very least what follows will show how certain uses of poststructuralism and postmodernism are repressive for the purposes of giving voice to marginalized concerns. I also hope this work will be suggestive of how we might borrow certain insights of poststructuralism and postmodernism to conceive a viable oppositional politics—a politics which, while it is sensitive to the fact of difference, does not exclude the importance of community.

1

Lyotard

All political theories begin from assumptions about the nature of the person and society. A political theory will be judged useful or true or convincing to the extent to which it matches one's background beliefs regarding the quiddity and parameter of the self and society. Given this view, it is my contention that an understanding, however cursory, of the structuralist and semiotic theory of the self is necessary to an understanding of postmodern political theory. The decentered subject, the centrality of difference and play, and the concomitant violence of unifying structures—themes which have their inception in the writings of Peirce and especially Saussure—are the foundation of postmodern thought.

These themes, however, are not always made explicit. Too often labels or concepts are adopted by postmodern theorists and critics without explanation to the reader why the self, or freedom, or oppression is being viewed in their particular way. Lyotard is one such obscurantist. He begins from a notion of a decentered self; for him the self can never be the author of meaning. Human beings are never the authors of what they tell, that is, of what they do—in fact there are never any authors at all.[1] But why not?

The disappearance of the self, the repudiation of the traditional notion of the subject as the bearer of meaning, is a result of a linguistic notion of the self, of seeing the self as something which is structured like a language. Lyotard believes that selves are "always already" presented as part of the social bond; they are always already a function of language[2] where language is not one monolithic discourse, but a multitude of different discourses without any grand narrative to connect the various language games; all there is is a heterogeneity of elements. This being the case, there is no reason to believe that stable language combinations can be established, nor is there reason to believe we can establish stable self-identities. This decentering of the self has

9

important consequences for social relations. For Lyotard the relation of self to others can only be an uneasy relation of unlike to unlike. Thus for Lyotard the principle of postmodern knowledge is "not the expert's homology, but the inventor's paralogy,"[3] and agonistics becomes the founding principle of social relations.

Given his commitment to the heterogeneous and open-ended nature of language and the self, Lyotard operates with the belief that any social theory which assumes that social (or cultural, or linguistic) elements are commensurate, or that the whole is determinate, will encourage a "regime of terror"; the impetus of social planners to operationality or commensurability or consensus will necessarily have terrorist overtones for it amounts to the threat: "Be operational [that is, commensurable], or disappear!"

Even in so brief a space, many of the themes of postmodernism have been sounded: the death of the author, the notion that the self is structured like a language and therefore heterogeneous and resistant of unity, the fiction of unifying structures in general, the impossibility of grand narratives, and the repressive and oppressive nature of technocratic society—to name but a few. But these themes are merely stated. Nothing has been explained. Without making explicit the assumptions with which he operates, as he often does not, Lyotard's propositions do not make much sense. Why, for example, does Lyotard view the self as a linguistic construct? Even if this model were appropriate, how could we get from the view of the self as essentially linguistic to the proposition that the self is fragmented, decentered, protean, and incomplete? Why are language games incommensurable and "not necessarily communicable"? Why are paralogy and agonistics appropriate models of social relations?

The answer to these and like questions only make sense against their appropriate backgrounds—which in this case is semiology and structuralism. I wish then to postpone my discussion of Lyotard and offer first a brief exploration of those structuralist and semiotic themes most relevant to an understanding of postmodern politics.

The semiotic and structuralist background

The two of us wrote Anti-Oedipus together. Since each of us was several, there was already quite a crowd. (Deleuze, *Anti-Oedipus*.)

The ubiquity of language

Semiotics calls to our attention the fact that we never encounter bare physical objects or uninterpreted data. We always and necessarily encounter objects and events already endowed with meaning. In other words, what we encounter are signs: we don't have objects on the one hand and thoughts or meanings on the other; it is rather that we have signs everywhere.[4] If we wish to understand our social and cultural world we must examine the network of relations which endow objects and events with meaning. Since language, be it written (Saussure) or spoken (the point of Derridian différance), is the primordial medium of an object, objects have meaning in virtue of their inscription in the linguistic network, or "signifying chain." This being the case, the objects of any science must be studied within the domain of discourse.

Arbitrariness and difference

The meaning of a signifier does not lie in a relation of representation, as a word to a thing, but in its difference from other signifiers. The signifier *gentle,* for example, gets its meaning from its difference from other signifiers of behavior such as *brutish* and *wild.* Or to use a more interesting and significant example, the signifier *black* has meaning only in contrast to the signifier *white.* This would mean that there are no natural race distinctions. This follows the lessons of Saussure: "A linguistic system is a series of differences of sound combined with a series of differences of ideas,"[5] and also, "language is a system of interdependent terms in which the value of each term results solely from the simultaneous presence of the others."[6] Thus, arbitrariness and difference stand as the two cornerstones of Saussure's semiotic theory: signification or meaning comes about in an arbitrary process of differentiation; every sign is inscribed in a chain or system within which it refers to other signs by means of the systematic play of differences. In the system of language there are only differences.

The decentered self

For my purposes the most influential part of Saussure's theory is that accepting the notion of language as a differential network and the principle of difference as the condition of meaning implies that there can be no origin of meaning, no "author." There can be no transcendental signified, no origin, no center, because the process of signification is infinite. This thesis amounts to an attack on Western metaphysics.

The traditional Western view assumes that the concept of structure implies a center, something which is at the heart of the totality and yet is also outside of it since it does not belong to that totality. This view goes back at least as far as the Parmenedes and the problem of participation of the Forms.[7] The possibility of a transcendental signified is, as Derrida notes, "ruptured," or disrupted, once attention is given to the structuring of structure, to the fact that meaning, i.e., language, exists as a signifying chain lacking a center. The center, he says, becomes a "sort of non-locus in which an infinite number of sign-substitutions come into play"[8] with the consequence that "a system in which the central signified, the original or transcendental signifier, is never absolutely present outside a system of differences . . . extends the domain of signification endlessly."[9] Since the domain, or "play," of signification has no limit, the full meaning of any concept is endlessly deferred. Instead of the metaphysical foci of Being and Truth, we have the Nietzschean substitution of play and interpretation. The field of language, to use Derrida's terminology, becomes the field of play, that is, the field of infinite substitutions. Substitutions are infinite because there is no center to arrest or ground the play of substitutions. The lack, or absence, of a center, or origin, permits this movement of play—or what Derrida also calls *supplementarity*.[10]

All of this bears on our understanding of the subject. Semiotic analysis decenters the subject. In the linguistic world the author of meaning disappears without identity into the field of differential play; the author of meaning becomes a "trace" in the linguistic act. The epistemological subject is therefore declared dead, or at least unknowable.

The political implication of difference

Just as the domain, or play, of signification has no limit, no natural closure, what is left of the subject is only infinite possibilities of interpretations within the linguistic chain; the subject is an open-ended narrative. But the differential network has another implication. Every presence defines an absence; at the same time as we say what it is we necessarily leave out of account what it is not. This points out the problem with closure or systems in general (hence Lyotard's equation of terror with social planning). The positing of structure cannot be reconciled with the ineliminable element of play, for the requirement of closure demands the repression of play even as play generates the structure. But this means that all definitions are necessarily incomplete. This will be true of any description of the self (as it will be for all other descriptions), for any description of the self represses its radical plurality.

The principle of difference and play is also the source of political commitment in postmodern theory, for the impulse to totalization (in this case, the demand to name the "I") is associated with totalitarianism, or for Lyotard, with "terror." Given the semiotic and structuralist background, the desire for closure as a guarantor of meaning and intelligibility can only be seen as an instrument of repression. In particular it represses the arbitrary nature of the origin or genesis by which a given structure is represented. Revealing that genesis would show the arbitrary nature of that starting point and would also remind one of the artificiality of beginning and end points. Foucault's notion of liberation will be seen to hinge on this belief, but it is more generally the mark of the postmodern notion of freedom—there is no fixed human nature since different narrative starting points would render us other than what we are.[11]

Language-shaping theory

Mine is not a thesis on the philosophy of language. It is not my intention to give a thorough exegesis or critique of contemporary semiotic theory—structuralist, poststructuralist, or otherwise. But we must not avoid the fact that Lyotard's acceptance of a particular view of language is determinant of his philosophical theory.

It has been necessary to touch upon the structuralist and poststructuralist view of language because it is my contention that such a view reveals the architectonic of Lyotard's thought: it is necessary for an understanding of his philosophy as a whole because it is what determines the shape of its parts. It is especially essential to an understanding of his view of the self, and it is this which in turn determines the form of his aesthetic and political ideals. Having then presented this outline, we are now in a position to undertake an examination of Lyotard, and we can return to those propositions which were merely stated above.

Lyotard's adoption of the structuralist/poststructuralist model is derived from the Saussurean/Derridian view which sees language as a plurality of heterogeneous and incommensurable "language games" or, as Lyotard comes to call it, "phrase regimens."[12] This background motivates, first, his move from the contention that the self is always and necessarily linguistic to the claim that this self is therefore essentially fragmented, decentered, protean, and incomplete—which in turn is determinate of both his aesthetic and political ideas of freedom and repression (terror)—and, second, also motivates his adoption of paralogy and agonistics as the appropriate model of social relations.

The postmodern theorist begins from the assumption that the structure of language radically determines our lives as human/social subjects. But "language" is here being conceived on the structuralist (poststructuralist) model described above. Lyotard understands human reality as being irreducibly mediated by language where language is understood as the differential system described by Saussure and amended by Derrida; the subjects born in language are structured by the differential logic of the signifying chain and kept unbounded, radically deferred, by the infinite variety of play and difference. The different elements of language are not commensurable, the whole is not determinable. It is therefore of the quiddity of language that its various functions are heteromorphous and so subject to heterogeneous sets of rules and expressions. This means for Lyotard both that different ways of using a single language will have separate rules appropriate to it and not to others so that, for example, the logic of prescription will not be appropriate to the logic of description, and also that "languages" very different from our own are equally worthy of being considered meaningful. As we shall see, this is important in his definition of terror and his corresponding view of justice: the goal is to recognize the voice of the Other, of those who have been victimized by the logic of the status quo, as speaking in a language as legitimate as our own. I say "to recognize the voice of the Other," but it must be pointed out that the voice of the Other can also reside in us; Lyotard's theory also gives liberation to those parts of us which have suffered in being made to conform to the standards demanded by the dominant voices in our society.

The self that shares in the nature of such language and is a function of heterogeneous, protean, and sometimes incommensurable language games having no grand narrative to unite them into a coherent whole is like language itself: decentered, protean, incomplete, and subject to fragmentation. The connection between language and the self is decisive for Lyotard's understanding of the self, for he views the self as a function of the infinite variety of language elements: as Lyotard says, human beings are "given in being made the addressee of any given speech act" (JG 36). The self is

> . . . dispersed in clouds of narrative language elements—narrative, but also denotative, prescriptive, descriptive, and so on. Conveyed

within each cloud are pragmatic valencies specific to its kind. Each of us lives at the intersection of many of these. However, we do not necessarily establish stable language combinations [not "necessarily" because there is no necessary structure to language or the self], and the properties of the ones we do establish are not necessarily communicable (PMC *xxiv*).

Lyotard thus views the self as a "territory of language," whatever is true of language will *eo ipso* be true of the human/social subject because there is no transcendental signified; all meaningful objects, the self being no exception, exist as part of the linguistic signifying chain and must be understood accordingly.[13] Since the subject, like any other meaningful object, is part of this linguistic system, and since this system has the attributes of being decentered, arbitrary, and incomplete, then so too must the subject be characterized as essentially fragmented, decentered, protean, and incomplete.

Lyotard operates on the belief that these four characteristics delimit the genuine (even if he would be uncomfortable using this word) nature of the self, and it is this self which his political theory is meant to protect and his aesthetic theory meant to celebrate. In general, his philosophy revolves around the attempt to protect the self against encroaching systems of unity and order which would force the subject to conform to artificial limits, structures, or modes of expression. The postmodern political project is dedicated to finding ways of presenting what has hitherto been unexpressed or silenced, or in Lyotard's terms, to finding ways of expressing or alluding to the "unpresentable." The task is to free expression from all subordinating logics, to put under suspicion what only yesterday has been received, to rejoice in "the invention of new rules of the game" (PMC 80). The task is one of "derealization" (PMC 78).

Lyotard's equation of consensus, commensurability, unity, homology, and efficiency with terror (which, along with his defense of paralogy, will be discussed in greater detail below) is at least understandable, if not necessarily defensible, once we recognize that his understanding of language and the self structured in this language commits him to defend what he calls the "pagan ideal"—an ideal which in my terminology amounts to radical pluralism.

Pagan politics

The pagan ideal is Lyotard's aesthetic affirmation of the diremptive self. It takes up the challenge he left us with at the end of *The Postmod-*

ern Condition: "Let us wage a war on totality; let us be witness to the unpresentable; let us activate the differences. . . ." (PMC 82).[14]

The aesthetic ideals of heteronomy, difference, and change that follow upon his view of the nature of the self have their political counterpart. Despite the fact that Lyotard finds difficulty in connecting the aesthetic with the political (a difficulty which is important and to which I will be returning[15]), I would argue that his aesthetics and his political views are codependent and that both are inseparable from his theory of the self; his aesthetic attitude as depicted in the pagan is expressive of both a (metaphysical) view of the self and of those political commitments formulated to protect such a self. Lyotard's commitment to change and the search for difference, for phrasing or embodying the unpresentable, is not merely an expression of an idiosyncratic preference, it is also prescriptive:

> There is no politics if there is not at the very center of society . . .
> a questioning of existing institutions, a project to improve them, to
> make them more just. This means that all politics implies prescrip-
> tions of doing something else than what is (JG 23).

Politics then is necessarily prescriptive, and Lyotard is very clear about both the fact that his writing is prescriptive and that it is political:

> I have always given myself as an excuse for writing a political reason.
> I have always thought I could be useful. Therefore, it ought to be
> obvious that I accept completely the idea that there is a prescriptive
> function to the idea of paganism (JG 17).

But the politics born in paganism is not unproblematic. Lyotard tells us that the principle of paganism is heteronomy and multiplicity, and the difficulties with founding a politics on this principle are many. These difficulties include, but are not limited to, the following: how fragmented, decentered, and changing can a subject be and still retain the qualities necessary to a citizen or political subject (or we might ask, how fragmented, etc., can language be and still yield anything resembling a "subject"—authorless or not?)? Or we could, as does Lyotard, phrase the question in terms of the problematic of judgment: paganism is defined as judging without criteria. But the question is how this kind of model enables one to get beyond judgments of pleasure (aesthetic judgments) to judgments of what is just or unjust (political judgments).

These problems are even more pronounced when we move to the level of social (political) interaction. If there is no unifying thread holding together a single subject, much less will there be the unity commonly thought to be necessary for the formation of political communities or groups or coalitions, and if there is no standard by which to judge the justice of individual actions or to adjudicate between competing desires/interest/actions on an individual level, how much more problematic is judgment on the level of collective decision making.

For Lyotard, the fact that the self constituted in the plurality of language games is not a unity means that it is necessarily heterogeneous (JG 36), having many, not necessarily coherent, interests—it is, in other words, radically plural. In the terms of this theory, proper names represent a heuristically useful, but a psychologically and socially artificial, convention since any name is made up of heterogeneous phrases taken from heteromorphous language games. It is this which makes the signification of the name open ended: "Phrases come to be attached to [a] name, which not only describe different meanings for it . . . and not only place the name on different instances, but which obey heterogeneous regimes and/or genres. Thus heterogeneity, for lack of a common idiom, renders consensus impossible. . . ." The extent to which Lyotard buys into the thesis of perspectivism leads him to argue that it is impossible to agree on what a name stands for, for what it stands for is always relative to the situation in which it comes up. This is true even for a name like Stalin: "The assignment of a definition to Stalin necessarily commits an injustice against nondefinitional phrases relating to Stalin, which this definition, for a while at least, ignores or betrays" (Diac 13).

But if there is no standard which could speak to the multifarious interests, desires—"personalities" if you will—of the schizophrenic self, there will also be no standard which could serve as an intersubjective (objective) or social (moral) guide or standard of judgment; "If all opinions are acceptable, then I cannot decide" (JG 81). And if the meaning of a name cannot be fixed, then moral judgments about what that name stands for or refers to is always a matter of opinion. Hence Lyotard's claim: "There is no politics of reason, neither in the sense of a totalizing reason nor in that of the concept. And so we must do with a politics of opinion" (JG 82). This has the consequence that for Lyotard consensus and community will necessarily be equated with the false imposition of unifying structure. It also determines the limits of justice: a just situation will be one in which all potential narrators are allowed to exercise their ability to narrate from their individual perspectives, where none of the narrative poles hold privilege over any other.[16] This demands of justice that it be a multiplicity.

Despite the immediate objections we might have to such a theory—after all, we may not want to be sanguine about the thesis that the meaning of "Stalin" cannot be fixed in any morally determinate way or that a debate about the virtues of fascism over democracy is merely a matter of opinion—it is important to see why Lyotard promotes it even at the expense of endangering the possibility of moral debate (of legitimation). Lyotard's thesis is that refusing to fix the boundaries of signification is the best weapon we have against the encroachment of control and domination, and it is such encroachments of terror that Lyotard is primarily concerned to battle.

Lyotard attacks terror from many angles: politically, as constituting injustice, aesthetically as stifling alternative expression. In *The Postmodern Condition,* his attack was against the normalizing structure of modern science. Here terror is primarily used to denote the Western model of science/rationality and the hegemony of techno-knowledge, which is built up around the performativity principle. In works like *The Differend,* his project is to analyze sociopolitical problems of justice in terms of the problem of language. Here he takes his stand by politicizing the linking of phrases. The view that phrases are linked in a way which belies strategic or political intent only makes sense against the background of Lyotard's poststructuralism and his unfortunate postmodern tendency to universalize difference—to see all and any structuring as "terroristic."

Take away the legitimacy of any grand narrative and what you have left can only be difference. Given that he believes that all language is a system of differential signs, he believes that language is undetermined. All determinations therefore, all ways of choosing to use language to build structure (and a phrase is an instance of such structure), amounts to an artificial and *strategic* imposition of an interested program. This is what lies behind Lyotard's claim that "the stakes bound up with a genre of discourse determine the linkings between phrases." He argues that "they determine them, however, only as an end may determine the means: by eliminating those that are not opportune. One will not link onto *To arms!* with *You have just formulated a prescription,* if the stakes are to make someone act with urgency. One will do it if the stakes are to make someone laugh" (D ¶148). Phrases are linked to procure success.[17]

Phrases and the linking of phrases are artificial and strategic. This is the case because, since language is a differential system, phrases and linkages always and necessarily exclude other possible phrases and linking of phrases (repress and suppress difference). Because Lyotard believes that every way of speaking suppresses other possibilities, that "every reality entails possible unknown meanings," he believes that language is always political: "Everything is political if politics is the possibility of the differend on the occasion of the slightest linkage" (D ¶192).

Lyotard's concept of "the differend" denotes the fact that something always remains to be phrased. The differend marks the case where the linking of phrases in a particular way becomes reified as the normal or rational or acceptable way of speaking—where phrases become "phrase regimens." Because other possibilities (voices) would exist if different linkages were permitted, phrase regimens institutionalize the silencing of the voice of the Other; the Other becomes a plaintiff divested of the means to argue and becomes, on that account, a victim.

Lyotard's political ideal is to give expression to those parts of our selves, or those voices, which have been marginalized or rendered inexpressible by the demands of unity and stability—demands which violate the heterogeneous nature of language and the self. This ideal is worked out throughout his writing. In his *Differend,* for example, he argues that one becomes a victim when one is divested of the means to argue. Thus injustice is equated with being silenced, not the least of which silencing is having one's difference keep one from being heard in the language of decision makers. Elsewhere Lyotard suggests the many ways one might be silenced:

> An injustice would be an injury accompanied by the loss of the means to prove the injury. This is the case if the victim is deprived of life, or of all his liberties, or of the liberty to make public his ideas of opinions, or simply of the right to testify to the injury, *or even more simply if the phrasing of the testimony is itself deprived of authority* [my emphasis]. In all of these cases, to the privation constituted by the injury there is added the impossibility of bringing it to the knowledge of others, and notably to the knowledge of a tribunal (Diac 5).

In general, then, Lyotard's pagan politics is tied to a philosophy of language which concentrates its critique on the linking of phrases. Linkage, the question of what will occur next after the occurrence of any phrase, is a political question, or rather it is already the question of the political in the form of the differend.

> In the differend, something asks to be put into phrases and suffers
> from the injustice of not being able to be instantly put into phrases.
> This is when human beings who thought they could use language
> as an instrument of communication learn through a feeling of pain
> which accompanied silence (and of pleasure which accompanied the
> invention of a new vision), that they are surrounded by language
> . . . to recognize that what remains to be phrased exceeds what they
> can presently phrase, and that they must be allowed to institute
> idioms which may not yet exist (Diac 7).

Because it is always possible to link phrases in alternative ways, the
choice of any particular linkage is a kind of "victory" of one over
another. Thus, conflict is built into the very nature of language (this
comes up in various guises and is also spoken of in the context of
"agonistics" and "paralogy"[18]):

> . . . a phrase comes along. What will be its fate, to what end will
> it be subordinated. . . . No phrase is the first. This does not only
> mean that others precede it, but also that the modes of linking
> implied in the preceding phrases—possible modes of linking there-
> fore—are ready to take the phrase into account and to inscribe it
> into the pursuit of certain stakes. . . . In this sense, a phrase that
> comes along is put into play within a conflict between genres of
> discourse. This conflict is a differend, since the success (or the valida-
> tion) proper to one genre is not the one proper to others . . . the
> multiplicity of stakes, on a par with the multiplicity of genres, turns
> every linkage into a kind of "victory" of one of them over others.
> These others remain neglected, forgotten, or repressed possibilities
> (D ¶183).

> There are as many different ways of winning as there are genres (D
> ¶186).

> You don't play around with language. And in this sense, there are
> no language games. There are stakes tied to genres of discourse.
> When these stakes are attained, we talk about success. There is
> conflict, therefore [and this] results from phrases (D ¶137).

When alternative linkings are not allowed to "speak," when it is
not recognized that "to link is necessary, but how to link is not," the
repression entailed in the victory of one phrase over another becomes
a form of terror.

Lyotard's concern with language is obviously political; his goal is
to see to it that "every injustice must be able to be phrased." The idea

of the differend makes it possible to consider the political as being a concern of all disciplines which find themselves linking and/or analyzing the linking of phrases. The irreverent pagan challenge to all disciplines is to forswear the limits imposed on meaning by the traditional criteria of rationality, or meaning, or cognitive prescriptions: "What is at stake in a literature, in a philosophy, in a politics perhaps, is to bear witness to differends by finding new idioms for them" (Diac 7).

It is also what is at stake for the historian: ". . . the historian must . . . break with the monopoly over history granted to the cognitive regimen of phrases, and he must venture forth by lending his ear to what is not presentable under the rules of knowledge" (Diac 14). The rules of knowledge are themselves a form of terror, and so what is called for in the pagan is to expand the very concept of "reality" into an essentially open-ended system.

It is the need for an open-ended system of knowledge—one which can include the differend, the unpresentable, can accommodate expressions foreign to the dominant phrase regimen—that is expounded in *The Postmodern Condition*. Here, as before, the text is motivated not only by political concerns, but also by the aesthetic need to promote the inventive self (although these are really two sides of the same coin).

The self which is radically undetermined by the infinite variety of play and difference is, in the words of Jameson, dissolved into a "host of networks and relations, of contradictory codes and interfering messages" (PMC *xviii–xiv*). Lyotard's need to protect and encourage free expression of this self leads him to champion "open systems"—"one[s] in which a statement becomes relevant if it 'generates ideas,' that is, if it generates other statements and other game rules" (PMC 64)— and to challenge all normalizing structures (stases) as being, wittingly or not, a form of terror. The terrorist system would be one which proclaims: " 'Adapt your aspirations to our ends—or else' " (PMC 63), which demands that everyone speak in a single voice.

By "terror" Lyotard means to denote anything which would contain or delimit the unbounded nature of the self. This would include forcing a single or particular definition or mode of expression on a subject (or decontextualizing legitimacy), for given the nature of the self we have been describing, to define would be to limit, and therefore, in Lyotard's terms, to terrorize. The "open system" model proposed by Lyotard, on the other hand, is prevented from being equated with terror because it possesses no general metalanguage in which all other languages could be transcribed and evaluated (PMC 64).

Pagan politics is then deeply committed to antiauthoritarianism in all forms and insists upon the aesthetic and political value of multiplicity and change, and the search for the unpresentable—for "legitimate" meanings expressed in ways that are not part of the mainstream language and so cannot as yet be heard (or "presented"). Lyotard sometimes (though he is not consistent in this) implies that these unpresented voices could, in principle, be heard. But, in fact, his thesis demands a stronger conclusion: they can never be presented. This is the consequence of his universalizing difference, and such a conclusion must, I shall argue, be rejected.

His insistence on "open systems" as the only system qualified to serve as the standard model of science, discourse, and knowledge, a system which would appropriately broaden its concept of legitimacy and rationality to include all modes of expression, sets him against thinkers like Habermas who retain a kind of Kantian optimism about the possibility of there being a "rational" community of mankind [sic].[19] Since language (and selves) is not homogeneous, it is not the case that it has only one interest or one overriding standard of rationality: "Genres are incommensurable, each has its own 'interests.' The 'force' of a phrase is judged by the standard of a genre's rules, the same phrase is weak or strong depending upon what is at stake. . . . Language does not have a single finality. . . ." (D ¶231).

For Lyotard the goal of dialogue cannot, and *must not*, be consensus: "Heterogeneity makes consensus impossible" (D ¶92)[20]; for consensus is "only a particular state of discussion, but not its end." Rather, the end must be paralogy, dissent. Whereas consensus closes off the unpresentable, paralogy allows its possibilities to remain open. Paralogy is thus endemic to the pagan ideal because it fights against the imposition of terror in all its forms by encouraging alternative ideas and modes of expression. For Lyotard "invention is always born of dissension." This is why *The Postmodern Condition* defines postmodern knowledge as the search for instabilities. He is seeking not to limit forms of expression, but to open us up to the unpresentable. As opposed to techno-knowledge or knowledge dominated by the performance principle, "postmodern knowledge is then not simply a tool of the authorities; it refines our sensitivity to differences and reinforces our ability to tolerate the incommensurable. Its principle is not the expert's homology, but the inventor's paralogy" (PMC *xxv*).

Hence paralogy is valued both for aesthetic reasons, it promotes the inventiveness of free spirits, and for its political usefulness, it makes us sensitive to, and tolerant of, difference.

We might well wonder in what the ideal of society can consist once we have adopted the model of paralogy and have given up on metanarratives and the possibility (or even desirability) of consensus. Lyotard conceives of the "Ideal of Society" as "a set of diverse pragmatics," a set which is "neither totalizable nor countable," the specific feature of it being that "the different language games that are caught up in the pagan universe are incommunicable to each other" (JG 58). By this last Lyotard means that the problems specific to one language game need not translate as problems, and certainly not in the same way, for another. Conflict resolution may not be possible, not only because the linking of phrases entails a victory of one way of linking over another, but also because understanding across group differences will not always be possible; the social web is made up of a multitude of encounters between interlocutors caught up in different pragmatics. But the heteronomous nature of language and the heterogeneous nature of linguistic rules means that there is no universal discourse underlying different language games, nor is there a single standard of rationality into which all discourses can be translated or from which all conflict could be measured. We have seen that this leads Lyotard to adopt a model of discourse (and of science and knowledge) based on paralogy—on dissent rather than consensus. But even granted that we agree to the inadequacy of models that retain universals and transcendental signifiers, we might still wonder whether the principle of paralogy gives us a workable model for communal interaction.[21] And if not, we might well question whether there is enough left of politics to serve as a meaningful—or acceptable—theory; can we have a politics that does not allow for structure?

Though I will argue that his theory fails to adequately deal with them, when pushed by Jean-Loup Thébaud, his interviewer in *Just Gaming*, Lyotard shows that he is aware of these kinds of difficulties. The following long passage is worth quoting both because it is an eloquent statement of the kind of pluralism his paganism engenders and of the difficulties it presents us with—and because it makes Lyotard culpable: he is aware that the consequences of his paganism must be addressed by any responsible political theory. But if Lyotard is really going to present us with a postmodern politics, his solution to the difficulties paganism engenders must nevertheless retain his pagan ideals. The quote that addresses the difficulties the postmodern insistence on the repudiation of structure and its valorizing of difference presents to a viable politics is as follows:

> . . . if one has the viewpoint of a multiplicity of language games, if one has the hypothesis that the social bond is not made up of a single type of statement, or, if you will, of discourse, but that it is

made up of several kinds of these games, . . . then it follows that, to put it quickly, social partners are caught up in pragmatics that are different from each other. And this multiple belonging, this belonging to several pragmatics, can manifest itself rather quickly. . . . Each of these language games operates a distribution of roles, if one can put it this way. Actually, it is even more complicated than that, because there are variants within the language games. . . . Actually there is, I would not even say a weaving, because a weaving requires a unity of thread, but a patchwork of language pragmatics that vibrate at all times. And that means that the partners, the people who are caught, occupy positions that are incommensurable to each other. Not only is there an incommensurability within a game between the position of recipient and that of utterer, for example, but from game to game, for the "same" position, there is incommensurability: it is not the same thing to be the recipient of a narrative, and to be the recipient of a denotative discourse with a function of truthfulness or to be the recipient of a command.

The picture that one can draw from this observation is precisely that of an absence of unity, an absence of totality. All of this does not make up a body. On the contrary. And the idea that I think we need today in order to make decisions in political matters cannot be the idea of the totality, or of the unity, of a body. It can only be the idea of multiplicity or of a diversity. Then the question arises: How can a regulatory use of this idea of political take place? How can it be pragmatically efficacious (to the point where, for example, it would make one decision just and another unjust)? *Is a politics regulated by such an idea of multiplicity possible?* [my emphasis] Is it possible to decide in a just way in, and according to, this multiplicity? . . . Can there be then a plurality of justices? Or is the idea of justice the idea of a plurality? That is not the same question. I truly believe that the question we face now is that of a plurality, the idea of a justice that would at the same time be that of a plurality, and it would be a plurality of language games (JG 93–95).

Pagan politics is offered as an answer to these questions. It constitutes Lyotard's suggestion for an alternative politics, for a politics which can be regulated by the idea of multiplicity. More on this will follow in the next section, where I discuss his idea of justice as a multiplicity. But his best intentions notwithstanding, the questions he poses remain outstanding, and to the questions posed by Lyotard I would add: Can the idea of justice be at the same time an idea of plurality? Can the idea of justice be placed under a "rule" [sic] of divergence rather than convergence (JG 95)? Can justice operate without community? Can politics regulate itself by the idea of plurality—can we have a genuine politics of difference?

All of these questions become pressing when evaluating Lyotard's pagan politics.[22]

We have seen that the model of science and knowledge which matches Lyotard's pluralist conception of the self is one which sees knowledge and science not, as would Habermas, as a search for consensus, but as a practice of paralogism. Paralogism legitimates a continued search for new moves which challenge the consensus of dominant paradigms— hence Lyotard's anti-authoritarianism. Here the quest is for instability, to undermine from within that very framework in which the previous "normal science" or model of rationality had been conditioned.

This principle of science, argued for in *The Postmodern Condition*, serves Lyotard as a model for the justice of society. Paralogism expresses his pluralism, his commitment to otherness and difference and it is used as the basic principle justifying openness to otherness in politics. The proliferation of "small narratives" both replaces traditional metanarratives of legitimacy and counters the logic of "performativity" (the term Lyotard uses for the dominant logic of societal rationalizations)—it serves, in other words, to counter terror. The political implication of this model as it relates to justice and the problem of judgment is the overriding theme of *Just Gaming* and *The Differend*, and it is the problematic part of the paralogistic model that interests me here. As Lyotard sees it, paralogism's denial of legitimating (and the legitimacy of) metanarratives leaves us in a politically dangerous position—it forces the kind of relativism whereby justice can only be a matter of judging by convention: "This is where there is an essential political problem . . . rule by convention would require that one accept, let's get to the bottom of things right away, even Nazism. After all, since there was near unanimity upon it, from where could one judge that it was not just? This is obviously very troublesome" (JG 74).

Despite his commitment to pluralism, his anti-authoritarian stance, and to the model of paralogy or the role of the pagan, his concern with the relativistic consequences of his thesis reveals the fact that he remains entrenched in the old paradigm which has at its heart the need for some kind of universalizing principle—in this case, of constraint; this becomes for Lyotard the problem of judgment, the problem of legitimation. Paralogism, he feels, must be regulated by normative constraints. In science, it is constrained by general criteria of progressiveness, especially expansion of the explanatory scope of theories and an increase in their predictive power. But the question he sets himself is, what is analogous to this in matters of justice? What, in short, constrains the plurality endorsed by paralogism? He is not, as he should be, satisfied with a (pagan) multiplicity of justices; he feels compelled to find a justice of multiplicity.

The questions posed by Lyotard at the end of the long passage above, especially those which worry the question of just vs. unjust actions and how to adjudicate between them, begin to hint at his uneasiness with the "cavalier" stance of the pagan. Lyotard's solution is to offer the "Kantian Ideal" as being that which works to constrain or regulate pagan justice. However, I will argue that this solution results in the downfall of Lyotard's political theory. Paganism and the Kantian Ideal cannot be reconciled. Lyotard's revitalization of Kantianism is a betrayal of his postmodern ideals and therefore forces us to reject him as a serious proponent of a politics of difference.

However this may be, there are useful insights to be found in a study of Lyotard's proposed paralogistic model and pagan attitude. I therefore begin the following section with what might be of interest to the postmodern political theorist. I suggest that his notion of justice as it takes shape against a background of radical pluralism is especially of such interest.

I have given an overview of Lyotard's paganism and have argued that we must understand his pagan theory of the self and language within the context of his commitment to a (post)structuralist theory of language. In the remainder of this chapter, I propose to discuss three aspects of Lyotard's political position in more detail: (1) his theory of justice, (2) the problem of pagan politics as it relates to judgment, and (3) his Kantian solution and why we must reject it.

Justice

Minorities are not social ensembles; they are territories of language. Everyone of us belongs to several minorities, and what is very important, none of them prevails. It is only then that we can say that the society is just. (Lyotard, *Just Gaming*)

Freedom and the justice of multiplicity

In *The Postmodern Condition*, Lyotard poses the following question: "Where, after the metanarratives, can legitimacy reside?" For Lyotard, the problem of postmodern justice is the concern to answer this question. As I shall argue, he has two incompatible answers. The first, compatible with his insistence on a multiplicity of justice, is genuinely innovative and in keeping with this commitment to pluralism. The second, resulting from his search for the justice of multiplicity, is regressive and belies his not yet outgrown conservativism.

If there are no grand narratives then neither can there be any universal rules. Another way of saying this is that there can be no prescriptions which are neutral between the heterogeneity of language games. This must be the case once it is recognized that far from being a unified whole, language is differentiated into distinct types of enunciations: prescriptives, interrogatives, speculations, etc., each of which has its own rules that constitute the various constraints that operate in any given narrative and are relevant only within its particular pragmatic context. When that context disappears, the instructions no longer make sense. Lyotard replaces the traditional notion of rules with "pagan instructions." These are not laws to be applied universally, since any such laws would be ignoring difference and hence would terrorize otherness, rather they are local indicators of what is appropriate within a given pragmatic context, and those instructions make sense only so long as they are tied to that context.

This notion of language and the scope of the domain of linguistic rules have the following impact on Lyotard's notion of justice: there are no universal rules to apply in cases of justice, no universal or context-free criteria of judgment; no "Gods." Instead of a single standard of justice ruling between different practices, there is only a multiplicity of justices each of which is peculiar to, and only has relevance within, its particular pragmatic context. Thus all voices would have equal legitimacy and would be free of the leveling impulse of grand narratives. *Legitimacy then is relative to the pragmatic context of localized narratives and as narratives are multiple, so too are criteria of legitimation.* This states in a nutshell his radical idea of justice as being a multiplicity.

This notion of a multiplicity of justices would be a genuinely pluralist notion of justice for it would militate against all the hierarchical privileging found in the tradition of grand narratives, against all "sacred cows." In her instructive review of Lyotard's *Instructions Païennes* (translated into English under the title *Just Gaming*) Cecile Lindsay fleshes out Lyotard's pluralist conception of justice (his paganism) in terms of a rejection of piety:

> This relativised vision of discourse leads to the rejection of . . . the *pious* attitude of belief or conviction that had made the dominant

response to the various 'grand narratives' of the past "a persistent piety for the passion of the true throughout history." A sustained effort at *paganism* would level all narratives, denying to any one narrative the privilege of speaking, or translating to others. Thus theoretical narratives such as those proposed by Marxism, speculative philosophy, aesthetics, or capitalism, fall from their place on the pious hierarchy and stand as equals among a virtually infinite set of competing conflictual alternative narratives.

One of the things this anti-pietism leads to is the rejection of the old conception of rationality as an overarching concept. Once one rejects grand narratives, legitimation can no longer reside in matching a single conception of what is rational or right.

This rejection of rationality challenges the West's traditional conception of justice with its claim to legitimization of its political and cultural hegemony, and it is precisely because pagan justice refuses all justification for imperialism and hegemony of whatever kind that Lyotard can claim that the adoption of his position makes us more sensitive to and tolerant of difference. No position can claim privilege, can claim to be more rational, more just, more humane. Rather, legitimacy resides in the recognition of and respect for the multiplicity and context-dependent nature of language games: each language game constitutes, to use Lyotard's phraseology, a "sovereign" realm, for the acknowledgment that any and all justifications are pragmatic and context-dependent relative to a particular language game forces the recognition of the sovereignty of each game, a recognition which will, he thinks, guarantee freedom and the elimination of repression. Each language game has its own rules by which a move made within (and only within) that game can be judged:

> . . . there is first a multiplicity of justices, each of them defined in relation to the rules specific to each game. These rules prescribe what must be done so that a denotative statement, or an interrogative one, or a prescriptive one, etc., is received as such and recognized as "good" in accordance with the criteria of the game to which it belongs (JG 100).[23]

Using the criteria valid to one language to judge another would violate Lyotard's principle of sovereignty, for any such intrusion of one language game upon the other is seen by Lyotard as revealing a totalitarian impulse toward stability and unity, impulses which militate against freedom. The scientific game of truth, for example, and the ethical game of obligation, constitute two different games and the "facts" revealed in one cannot be used to legitimate moves in the other.

There is, however, a difficulty with doing away with any regulations across different language games and identifying justice simply as a multiplicity of sovereign languages where the sovereignty of each language game is recognized. The difficulty is that there is nothing to preclude the natural pull of the imagination to expand its own territory thereby violating the sovereign boundaries of each individual language game. Such violations necessitate a different kind of justice, namely a justice of multiplicity, to police the multiplicity of justices. So freedom within each language game is only guaranteed, paradoxically enough, by the universal prescriptive that the multiplicity of justice (i.e., the singular justice of each game) be respected.

Thus, Lyotard's concept of justice as a justice of multiplicities intervenes to patrol the boundaries of each language game making sure that none attempt to regular another, and it is only in thus maintaining the sovereignty of each that genuine freedom can obtain and repression be eliminated. But this concept of justice does not only operate by imposing a universal value on all language games to respect the sovereignty of each, it also prescribes change as a universal value. "Justice . . . does not consist merely in the observance of the rules; as in all games, it consists in working at the limits of what the rules permit in order to invent new moves, perhaps new rules and therefore new games." (JG 100. See also 100–102) What the rules permit is invention and change, and though it is not clear how invention and new language games come about, this lack of specifics is intentional. The rules of invention cannot be prescribed since the rules must be ready to fit situations which, because they are context-dependent, are essentially open-ended. To limit the possibilities beforehand would be to remain within boundaries of the conventional. It is, however, clear what Lyotard's ideal of justice *proscribes*. What is never permitted, and what the justice of multiplicity is meant to insure, is the terror by which one game demands power over other games, setting itself up as sovereign not just within, but across language games. Such a move would do violence to multiplicity, and that can never be allowed.

Once again we see how his aesthetic ideals of heteronomy and difference have their political counterpart in his understanding of justice. A just society is one which guards the freedom to allow the proliferation of protean change and the invention and expression of new selves, and guards against terroristic moves which would force conformity and belittle inventive and even contradictory forms of expression.

Lyotard's pagan reconception of justice as multiplicity offers many attractions for the person committed to a politics of difference: this idea of justice expands the political sphere to include those whose voices have been silenced because they speak in terms other than those legitimated by the dominant model. In line with his picture of the diversity of language and his repudiation of metanarratives, along with the notion of a decentered self which follows upon this picture of language, Lyotard's ideal of justice as multiplicity calls to our attention the political nature of any theory which assumes unity and stability. Such theories may be terroristic, they may hide an urge to repress otherness. This possibility will haunt not only any theory which operates as if humankind were classifiable into finite and delineable categories tending toward universal agreement—as in, for example, the Enlightenment model of Rationality—but will also haunt any theory which would place boundaries on the protean nature of language. To the theorist of difference, one of the most striking consequences of the idea of a multiplicity of justices, because of its far-reaching and radical (and also potentially liberating) implications, is this possibility of calling attention to the imperialism of phrase regimens as *regimens;* again I would stress his insight that the linking of phrases is always political: ". . . thought, cognition, ethics, politics, history, or being . . . are all in play when one phrase is linked to another . . . the linking of one phrase to another is problematic and . . . the problem is the problem of politics. . . ." (D p. *xiii*).

The pagan notion of a multiplicity of justice thus (at least in theory) necessitates reconceptualizing politics as a politics of difference where otherness is not only expected, but encouraged. A just situation will be one which recognizes and allows all potential participants to have a voice, to narrate from their own perspective. This is what the recognition of the sovereignty of language games is at least meant to achieve. To define justice as a multiplicity is to prohibit the terror by which one system attempts to impose itself upon another, asserting itself as the dominant (correct) game. This would amount to a gross injustice because it would silence multiplicity and it is precisely this kind of injustice that Lyotard is working to prohibit.[24]

So at least on the surface, Lyotard's doctrine is politically liberating to those of us who would promote a politics of difference. However, on closer examination Lyotard's pagan model of a multiplicity of justices is also troubling. For example, we might well ask what the political and ethical force of his concept of justice is. For one thing, such a conception refuses the legitimacy of metanarratives and as we have already discussed, this has dangerous consequences: if "good" is equivalent to whatever one adopts, then justice (as well as morality) becomes a matter of the dominance of the strongest voice. But this is an outcome with which Lyotard is uneasy, an uneasiness which, as we shall see, leads to his downfall, for it leads him to adopt a kind of old-style (and regressive) Kantianism. Lyotard is not always pagan however; when he is not, he demands that legitimacy cannot reside in multiplicity. It demands a transcendent standard according to which multiple justices could be assessed, it wants to constrain the plurality endorsed by pluralism, to limit the definitions which could "legitimately" be placed on the definition of Stalin or Nazism. But, as I shall argue in the next section, the demand for a justice of multiplicity cannot be reconciled with the pagan celebration of a multiplicity of justices. And even less globally, Lyotard gets into trouble when he allows himself to be engaged in debate over what legitimates his (sometimes) theory that legitimation must be given up. Indeed, the whole notion of judgment might simply be captured by the idea of the multiplicity of justices—perhaps there is nothing further to look for—in which case relativism becomes a moot point.

The most widely recognized (and by Lyotard as well) of the problems engendered by the pagan model of justice is that it traps him in performative contradictions because he is not able, and also not willing, to give up the urge for grand legitimation: he oversteps the self-imposed limits of sovereign language games by claiming that his pagan notion of the multiplicity of language games can (must) be legitimated by the Justice of multiplicity. As Jean-Loup Thébaud, his interlocutor in *Just Gaming*, correctly notes, Lyotard can often be caught speaking like the "great prescriber himself" (JG 100). This problem is quite damaging, for in his attempt to legitimate his theory Lyotard allows idolatry (and Kant) in the back door, and in so doing gives up on his political commitment to difference.

Even more revealing of his inability to detach himself from the mainstream tradition in philosophy in the West is his worry that the relativism implicit in the pagan attitude leaves one impotent in matters of judgment. Whether or not one shares this worry depends on our understanding of judgment. Lyotard is not yet able, as I think Deleuze is, and Rorty at least claims to be, to take the leap of faith required to bring about the paradigm change from the tradition which worries about essentialisms to a genuine paganism which revels in Nietzschean perspectivism.

Most worrisome of all, however, is the conservativism implicit in Lyotard's proffered paganism.[25] Lyotard believes that a tolerance of difference will follow upon the admission of the sovereignty of language games: since each language game is sovereign, none has the right to intrude on another's territory. But this kind of doctrine does not necessarily give voice to difference (or give way to "greater sensitivity and tolerance") for at least two reasons. First, as critics of patriarchy know only too well, not all language games are equally empowered. Second, language games are not pacific, they usually, perhaps even necessarily, entail the intrusion into another's space, if for no other reason than that the social space is complex, it is made up of many *intertwining* language games.[26] In a society where both are true Lyotard's theory does nothing to change, or even challenge, the status quo. Lyotard's theory must address the political realities, otherwise the domination of the more powerful language games and its repressive power structure will remain intact and the voices of dissent will continue to be stifled—and hence, terror will continue to reign. This entails the claim that a merely formal notion of justice, one which does not take actual forms of oppression into account, must remain inadequate.

The problem of legitimation and the justice of multiplicity

I have suggested above that Lyotard's pagan notion of justice has a corresponding notion of injustice: namely the silencing of multiplicity. It is with this in mind that he demands the protection of the purity of language games. Justice involves respecting the sovereignty of genres and of keeping the question of prescriptions out of games other than its own, for "there is no genre whose hegemony over others would be just" (D ¶228). This becomes an issue where judgment is concerned, however, because we make judgments and "one judges not only in matters of truth, but also in matters of beauty (of aesthetic efficacy) and in matters of justice, that is, of politics and ethics. . . ." (JG 16). So Lyotard recognizes that in actuality we *do* make judgment across genres, but argues that this can be done in the absence of criteria and so still be in accord with the idea of the pagan. As David Carroll notes, Lyotard is attracted to Kant's *Third Critique* because he sees Kant as providing the argument that we can judge without criteria.[27]

For Lyotard postmodern politics demands not conformity to pre-established laws or systems and categories of thought, rather it demands a form of judgment that judges in the absence of determinate rules. Paganism then is a name "for the denomination of a situation in which one judges without criteria" (J 16). Within the pagan attitude no criteria can be found for speaking of morality and the public good (J 18). Yet he nevertheless insists on a particular "Idea of society":

> [The pagan] is simply the Idea of society, that is ultimately, of a set of diverse pragmatics (a set that is neither totalizable nor countable, actually). The specific feature of this set would be that the different language games that are caught up in the pagan universe are incommunicable to each other. They cannot be synthesized into a unifying metadiscourse (JG 58).

But in fact when it comes to matters of justice we do fudge with reference to criteria: the criteria of multiplicity. At one and the same time Lyotard wants to combine a radical commitment to otherness with a universalistic principle of constraint: paganism and the idea of justice as a multiplicity *prescribe* for all discourses that they respect the sovereignty of language games, and this involves Lyotard in a paradox, for he does what he insists cannot be done—namely with the idea of the Justice of multiplicity he introduces a universal principle of constraint. Many critics of Lyotard note this problem. Among them is Geoff Bennington, who sees the tension between the view of justice as a totality and the pagan idea of justice, which stresses dispersion and heterogeneity as being unresolved and damning for his theory of justice. He describes the paradox nicely:

> Games other than that of justice are just to the extent that they do not involve justice. Prescriptions must intervene in all games to make sure that it does not intervene on other games. The Idea of justice watches over the "purity" and propriety of all games, but in fact must prevent any such purity or propriety to the extent that it does watch over. Purity and propriety are rendered unthinkable by the requirement that prescription always already transgresses its own purity or propriety in a *pas au-delà* which intervenes to the extent that it forbids intervention (Geoff Bennington, "August; Double Justice," *Diacritics* Fall 1984, 69).

Ironically enough, Lyotard's own requirements make the justice of the Justice of multiplicity terroristic.

He attempts to get himself out of this dilemma, insisting that he does not mean (despite evidence to the contrary) that within the pagan there are no prescriptions. There are. But they are not grounded in anything, and that is supposed to make all the difference:

> There are prescriptions in the pagan! It is fundamental even. . . . There always are prescriptions; one cannot live without prescriptions. . . . I believe that one of the properties of paganism is to leave prescriptions hanging, that is, they are not derived from an ontology. This seems essential to me (J 59).

But what if the pagan philosopher is forced to consider certain questions like the ones Jean-Loup Thébaud asks of Lyotard: "What do we do with a thesis like 'it is unjust; I rebel'? How is one to say this if one does not know what is just and what is unjust? If the determination of the just is the object of a perpetual sophistic debate? And yet, in everyday life, everybody says, 'It is unjust' " (JG 66). When is an obligation, a law, an act, unjust? What is it to *be* unjust? Can there be answers to these questions in the pagan? (Can we found a politics on a theory which refuses the legitimacy of such questions?)

First one must say that Lyotard accepts the legitimacy (the force) of these questions, questions which would seem at any rate to presuppose the need for criteria, for a "grounding." Despite various statements to the contrary, he is uncomfortable with politics being founded on opinion. What he should say is that since any and every minority can be just, the only injustice will be that no minority is to prevail upon any other—period (and still this would entail a seemingly illegitimate prescription, viz., what is the status of *this* claim.)

But paganism notwithstanding, he sees this attitude as unacceptable. First, it presents a problem of judgment: "How do I decide among opinions if I no longer accept as legitimate the appeal to science? Where do I get this capacity to judge? If all opinions are acceptable I cannot decide" (JG 81).

Second, it raises the question of legitimation. Even if one respects the sovereignty of language games, the purity of genres, one must still discriminate between just and unjust prescriptions. As Thébaud notes, the "Idea of justice" which Lyotard introduces to guarantee the justice of multiplicities actually begs this more fundamental question: even if the Idea of justice is successful in its goal of keeping prescriptions, narration, description, etc., in their "proper" order, "once the games have been restored to their purity, one must still discriminate between just and unjust prescriptions" (JG 96). Lyotard agrees that this is a necessity, but as yet he has failed to provide the criteria for judgment.

Kant and the betrayal of paganism

But is such hesitation vain?

In the section above we have seen Lyotard refuse the adequacy of the model of justice proposed by the pagan, namely, that in the absence of metanarratives, legitimacy or justice becomes that which has been judged to be just and upon which everyone within the parameters of a language game (community?) agrees. He claims that such a model is inadequate, for "under those conditions there is not the possibility of politics. There is only consensus. But we know what that means: the manufacture of a subject that is authorized to say 'we' " (JG 81).

That paganism makes of politics a matter of opinion or convention flags for him its "bad side"—"indifferentism" (JG 96). Despite what one might have expected from the formal notion of justice put forth in the pagan which requires that genres be kept pure, he agrees with his interlocutor that "one cannot simply be indifferent to the content of the language game" (JG 96). But the criteria of legitimation cannot be found in the pagan; to legitimate the Justice of multiplicity, to legitimate prescriptions of the just and unjust, he has to go outside the restrictions required by the pagan—to Kant. And not to the Kant of the *Third Critique*, but to the Kant of the *Second Critique* and a kind of categorical imperative. And this gives the game of justice the distinctive, and according to the pagan, illegitimate, feature of including a finality, an Idea . . . a transcendence: "There is a transcendence of justice" (JG 69). This transcendence takes the form of a categorical imperative: "in matters of justice, act in such a way as to regulate all your actions to be in conformity with the idea of multiplicity" (see JG 94–95). Thus, it turns out that the moral law Lyotard seeks is one that has within it the criteria of universal legislation, and this entails, as he is forced to admit, the return of the idea of unity and totality (JG 94–95). It is also importantly a reneging of his aesthetic ideal for the moral law demands conformity, even if it is conformity to the Idea of Multiplicity.[28]

But if this is the end result of his project, then we are forced to conclude that he fails in his attempt to offer a progressive political model, one which could be used to build a politics of difference. In his disavowal of aesthetic (pagan, postmodern) politics, and his insistence on the need for a regulatory ideal, he resurrects the idea of justice as the domination of one game over others: ". . . the justice of multiplicity . . . is assured, paradoxically enough, by a prescriptive of universal value. It *prescribes* the observance of the singular justice of each game. . . . It *authorizes* the "violence" that accompanies the work of the imagination. It *prohibits* terror . . . [all emphasis mine]" (JG 100). And it does so under the auspices of Kant: "If we remain with opinion [that is, within the aesthetic realm of the pagan] what will be just is ultimately that upon which people agree . . . is just. It is common opinion. That is an extraordinarily dangerous position. If, on the contrary, we take a Kantian position, we have a regulator, that is a safekeeper of the pragmatics of obligation" (JG 76).

But why must we see the pagan as yielding an "extraordinarily dangerous position"? Rorty's suggestion is that this conclusion is a result of Lyotard's worry over the relativistic consequences of his thesis, and maintains that this worry betrays the fact that Lyotard is not able to abandon the modernist demand for legitimation. He may be right. But as we shall see, though Rorty is more self-conscious than Lyotard, he is no more successful in maintaining the position he pretends his radical politics requires.

At any rate, we finally have an answer to a question asked earlier—what constrains the plurality endorsed by paralogism is the Kantian Idea: morality is regulated by the "Idea" of a "horizon of reasonable beings . . . that can exist together and form a totality." The Idea allows Lyotard to protect the normative value of the maximization of diversity or multiplicity. What is unjust becomes that which impedes the multiplicity or diversity of small narratives, that which would dominate or terrorize.

But this answer will not do, for it does not allow us to get beyond the Enlightenment conception of reason or the "modernist demand for legitimation." This is the case because his hesitation *is* between two incompatible positions. Try as he might, paganism cannot be reconciled with Kantianism as is evident by the end of *Just Gaming,* where, contrary to all prohibitions of the pagan, he ends by speaking in the voice of the "great prescriber himself."

That in the final analysis he chooses to regulate his paganism by the Kantian Idea forces the following conclusion: either his paganism actually does not ground a viable alternative to traditional hegemonic politics, or the fault is not with the pagan ideal per se, but with Lyotard's lack of courage to embrace the radical position it necessitates (as would be Rorty's contention).

Given the former possibility we need to ask, what are the consequences of the pagan for politics? In his more "mature" (meaning non-pagan) voice, Lyotard claims that politics demands judgment act as a regulative ideal. Pagan politics fails, however, to meet this requirement because it is equivalent to "a kind of aesthetic politics"; pagan politics offers only aesthetic judgment as the standard for discriminating between the just and the unjust. But "it is not true that one can do an aesthetic politics. . . . Aesthetic judgment allows the discrimination of that which pleases from that which does not please. With justice, we have to do, of necessity, with the regulation of something else" (JG 90).

But this repudiation of aesthetics is highly problematic—not just for Lyotard, but for the viability of postmodern politics in general. In the postmodern political program aesthetics cannot be divorced from politics, for it is the aesthetic attitude which demands multiplicity, invention, protean change, etc. Repudiate the requirements demanded by the postmodern aesthetic and you will also have allowed for the reinstantiation of a politics which demands consensus, finality, performativity . . . all those things which work toward silencing genuine diversity.

On the other hand, we must take seriously the possibility that a politics built upon the demands of the postmodern aesthetic is too problematic to be acceptable; it must be able to admit some model of consensus and community, even if it is not the traditional one.

Lyotard begins from the assumption that consensus is a sign of cooption or terror, of the imposition of order on multiplicity. Since he understands plurality to be the mark of the subject, he views what he sees as the homogeneity presupposed by the politics of community (of "a" or "our" tradition) to be necessarily repressive, for it both forces and enforces the marginalization of anything nontraditional (or accepts it by making difference work for the status quo. The acceptance of the Other usually entails a perversion of the original intent, as for example, when "Do the right thing" becomes a byword on the floor of the Senate). Lyotard is here pointing to something which needs to be taken into account. When victims are made to speak in one voice, when "rationality" is viewed as a fixed model, as a necessary goal, then it is inevitable that voices of difference will be silenced. In such cases silence may be the only, even if ineffective, form of protest, for to be understood would already be to be coopted. But it is a less than potent form of protest, and by insisting on paralogy rather than consensus, rationality can be made part of the debate in a way that Habermas's model, for example, would not allow.

The repudiation of community, then, can come out of a desire to broaden the political base. It disallows the traditional way of dealing with serious dissension—as when with Rousseau one claims the right for "majority" rule by offering as a mark of its non-repression the fact that those who are in disagreement are always free to leave.

The problem with Lyotard's view, however, is that it assumes that consensus must necessarily be a mark of terror. But it could also be a mark of genuine agreement. Agreement need not be based on terror, and in fact the segregation Lyotard requires with the autonomy of language games might itself be seen as a mark of terror. The thesis of the autonomy (sovereignty) of language games does not *allow* us, for example, to consider the thesis of the ubiquity of power, viz., that power may in fact already impede on many spheres other than the one specific to the game of prescription. Power does not remain tied to a specific genre. This is the liberating insight of Foucault's work, and also indicates the need to be wary of the neat division of spheres— as for example the public and the private; when critically examined, such separations often serve to mask the domination of power regimes. What is needed is a theory which respects difference while also allowing an open-minded examination of sameness. Sameness (unity) might be the end result of a successful, but illegitimate co-option of power. But it might also be the mark of genuine similarities. Consensus cannot simply be ruled out of court. As Lyotard himself sees (and in so seeing repudiates his paganism), consensus is not simply the silencing of multiplicity; it is also necessary for a viable politics. Unfortunately, as he conceives of the role of the aesthetic, it becomes impossible to retain the possibility of consensus—and so of community—and still remain faithful to his radical commitments. But whether Lyotard's failure is a result of a problem endemic to any aesthetic (postmodern) politics remains a question which will be taken up in the following chapters.

Can we have an idea of consensus which at the same time respects multiplicity? In my final chapter I shall argue that these two ideas are compatible as long as we ground a politics of difference in a protean understanding of "subjects-in-community." But Lyotard is not so in-spired. Instead of looking ahead at new possibilities for answering this question in the affirmative, he goes back to the traditional Kantian scheme and so loses the game. A politics regulated by the idea of multiplicity is not possible within Lyotard's system because he offers Kant as the model, and this is a model which simply is recalcitrant to the radical multiplicity demanded by the postmodern aesthetic and a politics of difference.

Previously he has argued that the heteromorphous nature of language games make these games subject to heterogeneous sets of pragmatic rules and so make it impossible for all speakers to come to agreement on which rules or metaprescriptions are universally valid. He has also argued that the goal of dialogue cannot be consensus since its end must be paralogy. These two arguments taken together work to argue against the belief that humanity can be viewed as a collective (universal) subject seeking its common emancipation through the regularization of the "moves" permitted in all language games and that the legitimacy of any statement resides in its contributing to that emancipation. And yet, in the final analysis, when faced with "indifferentism," which is the bad side of paganism, when faced with questions about how there can be prescriptions within the pagan, he gives up on the difficult and radical position articulated by the pagan and gives in to the conservative demand for the legitimization of rights talk.

This points out the unacceptable paradox resulting from the need he feels for a transcendent Idea as the regulator of the multiplicity of local justices. He turns to the Kantian Idea of Freedom to regulate this idea of justice, believing that this Idea can be admitted by the pagan because this regulating Idea does not dictate what we should do in any particular case since it is merely formal and has no content (JG 85). It demands only that the future of further inquiry always be kept open: "act in such a way that the maxim of your will may erect a principle of multiplicity," or, "act in such a way that the whole of rational beings may be preserved."

But the reason Lyotard feels the need to resort to the Kantian Idea in the first place is not that he wants an *idea* to be regulated, but because he feels a need to regulate *action*. In fact he feels that politics needs to have objective (and I mean "objective" in the Kantian sense) criteria for deciding *"this* is just, *that* is not," or it cannot be properly said to be a politics at all: "there cannot be a politics of opinion." But even supposing the Idea is one of multiplicity or diversity, can such an Idea have practical efficacy to the point where it could make a difference politically, to the point where it could be used to make one decision just and another unjust? He is looking for a way of legitimating such decisions beyond conventional agreement, but can the Idea of Freedom do this without violating its very principle? Lyotard refuses to face the fact that it cannot, that the pagan and the Kantian represent two mutually exclusive positions. He cannot simply answer the question of the violation of multiplicity by the Idea by saying as he does, "And here I don't know" (JG 94), for he does know really, just as really he knows his "hesitation" is not vain: "As soon as you say 'always act in such a way that the maxim of your will may be erected into a principle of universal legislation' one falls back into the horizon of unity and totality" (JG 94–95).

The issue is one of *practice* (praxis) and therefore of politics. Lyotard tries to imagine an idea of justice that would at the same time be that of a plurality—and such a concept of justice will be needed by a politics of difference—but the idea of justice he imagines is required comes out of a tradition which cannot accommodate his paganism.

The problem with basing legitimacy on the universalization of maxims is that however they are phrased they always demand a horizon of unity and totality. Let us begin with Lyotard's mildest statement of the maxims to be used in deciding on the justness of an action (or at least on which maxims cannot be moral [JG 74]): negatively, "act in such a way that the maxim of your will may not be erected into a principle of universal legislation"; or positively, "act in such a way that the maxim of your will may erect a principle of multiplicity" (JG 94). Even such mild versions call up Enlightenment views proscribed in the pagan; it demands convergence and a horizon of unity and totality, and so denies the legitimacy of any (or all) maxims—some ways of acting will be more just than others, and that according to a prescription not immanent to the rules of that language game. Justice is here being placed under a rule of convergence rather than divergence; one game dominates upon others. Both oppose the pagan prohibition of terror and its concomitant demand for justice.

Furthermore, these maxims assume what is explicit in bolder formulations, namely it presupposes a universal community of rational beings or a unity of humanity (JG 93), and despite the fact that he struggles with the incompatibility of the regulative Idea and his pagan prescriptions (see, for example, JG 76), in the end he adopts a unity of humanity, of a universal community, as his regulating Idea: as with Kant, for Lyotard too a community of ethical phrases is possible, given the idea of universal humanity; I's and you's are exchangeable (D p. 125). Although the viewpoint of a multiplicity of language games would militate against the Idea of a unified community, the moral Kantian imperative Lyotard adopts demands that we act as if our maxim of action was supposed to be a law of a community of "reasonable beings" (D p. 127): "act so that your maxim is in accordance with the whole of reasonable beings."

So we see that Lyotard's Kantianism forces the repudiation of his condemnation of universality and totality, and so reneges on that which was liberating to a politics of difference: namely the Idea of justice as a multiplicity, of a politics based on a rule of *divergence* rather than convergence.

And for one who hopes to find a grounding for a politics of difference, all attempts to reconcile his paganism with his Kantianism only serve to make matters worse. In particular we can look at an attempt which makes unbelievable the claim that his theory makes us more sensitive to, and tolerant of, difference.

To illustrate this I take as an example Lyotard's attempt to account for how the prescriptive can obligate across language games/differences. This entails a defense of the transcendence of the Idea:

> *JFL:* What is called the transcendence of the prescriptive is simply the fact that the position of the sender, as authority that obligates, is left vacant. That is, the prescriptive utterance comes from nothing: its pragmatic virtue of obligation results from neither its content not its utterer.

> *JLT:* And so it is because the recipient is taken ahold of, it is because one is taken ahold of by something that is beyond us that there is obligation. Or better: it is because it is beyond us and because it takes ahold of us that there is obligation (JG 72).

But in thus defending the transcendence of the Idea, in thus aligning himself with the Kantian (Rawlsian) tradition that requires that in universalizing the maxim one must abstract from one's particular heteronomous nature, in acting as if one *can* listen objectively, neutrally, etc., Lyotard does not simply not provide us with a means of evaluating difference, he more insidiously removes the possibility of genuine critical analysis—of questioning authority. If there is one lesson of the postmodern/poststructuralist that must be incorporated into any forward-thinking political theory, it is the fact that there is no neutral standpoint. Prescriptive utterances always come from a particular standpoint, and justice must demand an evaluation of that context, both for the values endemic to that particular standpoint, and also to see how it effects other possibilities. But Lyotard forecloses on such evaluation.

Lyotard likens the language of prescription to a game in which no one is talking. He argues that the position of the sender is "neutralized," for "only if it is neutralized will one become sensitive not to what is, not even to the reason why it says what it says, not even to what it says, but to the fact that it prescribes or obligates" (JG 71).

But we cannot allow Lyotard to reinstate the myth of the neutral standpoint. The law which Lyotard refuses to say where it comes from and in respect to which I insist we cannot be neutral, itself cannot be neutral. And here "neutrality" is a mask behind which all manner of domination might lurk. And he allows us no possibility of unmasking.

In Kant's formulation of the Categorical Imperative we remain autonomous because the moral law is a law we give ourselves. Lyotard does not fall into the trap of subscribing to the Kantian notion of autonomy, but ironically enough, in attempting to distance himself from Kant's position, in refusing to say where the law *does* come from, his thesis is even less acceptable than Kant's. Neutralizing the position of the sender takes away the point of questioning and would have us simply obey: "For us, a language is just and foremost someone talking. But there are language games in which the important thing is to listen, in which the rule deals with audition. Such a game is the game of the just. And in this game one speaks only inasmuch as one listens, that is, one speaks as a listener, not as an author."[29]

But such a position is unacceptable to a politics of difference; a politics which would have us be more sensitive to and tolerant of difference must allow for the discursive redeemability of prescriptions. In placing the Idea of Justice outside of the realm of the knowable, outside what can be critically questioned and examined, Lyotard makes justice a form of the unjust. In matters of justice listening is never enough.

2

Rorty

Can postmodernism remain true to the ideals of radical pluralism it borrows from the poststructuralist critique of language and the self and at the same time accommodate such pluralism within a new political program? Can postmodern politics engender a *politics* of difference?

I claim that it cannot do so if it is unable to allow room for consensus, community, or solidarity—though we need to understand these terms as something dynamic and essentially open to change, regroupings, and realliances. Such a reconceptualization is in keeping both with the demands of poststructuralism and, as I shall argue, with oppositional politics.

This claim will be developed in the final chapter. For the moment, let me foreshadow that discussion with the following unsubstantiated thesis: solidarity is necessary both for self-understanding and empowerment. Here I will claim, contrary to many interpretations of poststructuralist critical theory, that pluralism both needs and is able to accommodate a sense of self-identity, and self-identity in turn requires identity with others. The picture I have in mind is as follows: sometimes we recognize parts of ourselves in the stories of others. When we do, and when enough of us do, then we feel solidarity and begin to be able to formulate a vocabulary for our oppression, and hence have the tools ready for structuring our liberation. Out of this solidarity, which need not, it is important to note, ignore significant and perhaps even ineliminable differences (identity can have strategic value), we are able to build points of resistance. Without solidarity we are powerless not only to effect change, but even to have a critical sense of ourselves as beings constructed within matrices of power.

Let me be clear. A politics of difference is concerned with opening up a space for oppositional movements; the political impetus toward a politics of difference is the self-determination of marginalized groups.

What I would add and insist on is that such movements cannot be formulated without the accommodation of some, though not the traditional, notion of consensus, community, or solidarity. These terms will have to be reconsidered—in difference to the Enlightenment tradition and in deference to the Nietzschean/Derridian one—as essentially unstable. Just as it is a mistake to universalize totality, so too is it a mistake to universalize difference.

In their own ways, both Lyotard and Rorty fall into this trap.

We have seen that Lyotard falls into it by becoming entrapped in the following false dichotomy: either relativistic pluralism or terroristic consensus.[1] He universalizes difference with the consequence that he is unable to conceive of consensus and community as anything other than totalizing and hence terroristic.

Rorty would seem to be an advance over Lyotard if only because he rejects these dichotomies. I will argue, however, that he does so unsuccessfully; his pluralism rejects relativism at the expense of a kind of cavalier elitism, and his politics makes room for solidarity only by imposing a form of terror; his public/private distinction forces the notion that only one form of political discourse, the liberal democratic one, is valid.

Thus, although Rorty might at first seem to offer us a workable postmodern politics because he claims to succeed where Lyotard could not—he claims to be able to retain a notion of radical plurality necessary to the postmodern aesthetic *and* a concept of solidarity that I claim is necessary to political theory—in fact his vision of postmodern politics fails as well. Rorty is subject to a form of the same charge he levels against Lyotard: if Lyotard's project fails because it is unable to give up the modernist demand for legitimation, Rorty can be charged with being unable to give up the modernist demand for totality. I shall argue that Rorty's idea of solidarity harbors that which Lyotard warns against in his discussion of consensus, namely a kind of universalizing of totality which amounts to terror. Insofar as this is the case, he can, in line with a Lyotardian critique, be viewed as an apologist for cultural imperialism. Rorty's vision of politics cannot serve oppositional politics.

Before I substantiate this charge, I wish to iterate the ways in which Rorty claims to be able to avoid Lyotard's dichotomies, dichotomies which, I have argued, have kept Lyotard from being able to offer a viable model of postmodern politics. How can we have non-relativist pluralisms and non-terroristic consensus? Rorty's "solution" is most exhaustively laid out in his book *Contingency, Irony, Solidarity*, and so my discussion is mostly focused on that work.

Non-relativist pluralisms; poeticized culture

The simplest statement of Rorty's solution to the worry that radical pluralism ("paganism" in Lyotard's terms, "irony" in Rorty's) leads to relativism would claim that the worry over relativism makes sense only within the context of Modernist or Enlightenment vocabularies. Once these vocabularies are given up, the worry over relativism makes no sense, indeed, the question does not even arise. These are vocabularies that he, but not Lyotard, has abandoned.

In his articles on the contingency of language, the self, and community[2], Rorty argues that radical pluralism will be seen to harbor vicious relativisms only so long as one retains the Enlightenment expectation of rationality and subjectivity and Modernist beliefs in things like human essences or grand legitimating narratives. Those of us who feel compelled to answer charges of relativism are implicitly accepting the notion that there are criteria to appeal to beyond the pragmatics of our situation or our particular game. In contrast to this view, Rorty argues (in line with Wittgenstein and Davidson) that truth is a property of sentences, and since sentences are dependent for their existence upon vocabularies, and since vocabularies are made by human beings, then so are truths (CIS 21). Truth is thus a causal or contextual question, rather than one about the adequacy of representation or expression.

Rorty thus denies that the questions motivated by worries of relativism, questions like "Is the language we are presently using the 'right' language?" make sense, for such questions presuppose that there is some third thing which stands between the self and reality. This presupposition assumes what Rorty denies, viz., that there are nonlinguistic things called "meanings" which it is the task of language to express, as well as the idea that there are nonlinguistic things called "facts" which it is the task of language to represent. Both ideas are rejected because they perpetuate the idea of language as a medium (CIS 13). By contrast, Rorty insists that the human self is created by the use of a vocabulary rather than being adequately or inadequately expressed in one, and that just as the self is always open to redescription, so too are the things we say of it. He is aware that such a position leads him to accept that anything could be made to look good or bad, important or unimportant, useful or useless, by being redescribed. This bespeaks his commitment to a radical Nietzschean or Bloomian pluralism, to "ironism." But whereas a similar consequence of Lyotard's paganism led Lyotard to worry about the consequences of its political and moral implications, Rorty refuses to allow that pluralism forces such worries because he rejects, in a way that Lyotard did not, the baggage attached to the sense of these concerns, namely, he rejects the idea that the world or the self has an intrinsic nature: "Finite, mortal, contingently existing human beings cannot derive meaning of their lives from anything except other finite, mortal, contingently existing human beings" (CIS 45). Once the idea of grand narratives is really given up and the vocabulary of self-creation is put in its place, relativism has no context and serves no purpose (CIS 8).

Rorty's claim that the truth is not "out there" might seem to lead him into the relativistic position he is claiming to abandon—but he refuses this charge. Radical pluralism, which in Rorty's case amounts to a belief in the "radical diversity of private purposes, of the radically poetic character of individual lives, and of the merely poetic foundation of the 'we-consciousness' which lies behind our social institutions" (CIS 67–68), need not be a relativist position. The distinction between relativism and absolutism, rationality and irrationality, morality and expediency, is a remnant of vocabularies which the pluralist no longer finds useful. He would replace this vocabulary with one which uses the metaphor of self-creation (hence his valorization of the "strong poet"), and argues that this is better suited for the purposes of presenting and furthering democratic society.

Rorty offers no argument in the traditional sense in his defense. Indeed he could not, for to do so would force him to participate in a debate which presupposes that we can search for legitimacy in something outside of our immanent practices. For Rorty, morality is a language, which means that it is the result of accepting certain metaphors as useful. Our moral vocabulary is always open to redescription, and the description one chooses will depend upon one's particular purposes, purposes that can never be theory neutral. For Rorty, giving up such notions as relativism also entails giving up the ideas of neutrality, objectivity, and justification—if by justification we mean to appeal to something other than contingent practices. There can be no presuppositionless critical reflection conducted outside of a particular linguistic and historical context. One always speaks from an interested standpoint. The question, therefore, "How do you know?", must be refused and replaced with questions like "Why do you talk that way?"

As soon as Lyotard enters into discussion with Thébaud over the justification of his position, as soon as he accepts that relativism might be a valid concern for the pagan, he loses the game. The question assumes that some theory-neutral standpoint is possible.

Rorty, on the other hand, insists with Joseph Schumpeter that "[t]o realize the relative validity of one's convictions and yet stand for them unflinchingly, is what distinguishes a civilized man from a barbarian" (CIS 46).[3] He categorically denies that neutrality is an option, but this does not worry him; neutrality is not a desideratum:

> . . . neither Schumpeter's phrase "relative validity" nor the notion of a "relativist predicament" will seem in point if one grants Davidson's claim that new metaphors are causes, but not reasons for changes in belief, and Hesse's claim that it is new metaphors which have made intellectual progress possible. If one grants these claims, there is no such thing as the "relativist predicament," just as for someone who thinks that there is no God there will be no such thing as blasphemy. For there will be no higher standpoint to which we are responsible and against whose precepts we might offend. There will be no such activity as scrutinizing competing values in order to see which are morally privileged. For there will be no way to rise above language, culture, intuitions, and practices one has adopted and view all these as on a par with all the others. As Davidson puts it, "Speaking a language . . . is not a trait a man can lose while retaining the power of thought. So there is no chance that someone can take up a vantage point for comparing conceptual schemes by temporarily shedding one's own (CIS 50).

Thus, Lyotard's search for an Idea of Justice over and above the multiplicity of justices is evidence of the fact that he was unable to give up the idea of philosophical foundations repudiated in his disavowal of grand narratives. Rorty's "poeticized culture," on the other hand, amounts to a simple acceptance of a multiplicity of justices and the sovereignty of the pragmatics of language games, and he accepts that such a view forecloses on the possibility of grounding such multiplicity in an Idea of Justice. Rorty's notion of a poeticized culture, a culture whose history, customs, morality, and desires are a function of the fact that certain poets of the past spoke as they did (CC 13–14), appears to offer a radical pluralism which refuses, in a way Lyotard did not, the sense of the charge of relativism. But as we shall see, the strong poets do not lend themselves to the ideals of a liberal politics; and there still remains our other problem: the choice between solidarity or terror.

Poetry or politics?

The aesthetic which Rorty is committed to is a Nietzschean one that valorizes irony, play, and protean change. The self appropriate to such an aesthetic is a self conceived of as a centerless random collage of contingent and idiosyncratic needs (FMR 12). There is no single or correct description of the self. Neither is there a human essence uniting distinct individuals, or any one thing called justice, or rationality, or truth. There can be no "correct" way of acting, no "ought" determining hierarchical modes of existence.

This view of the self encapsulates the substance of Rorty's ironism. It is a view which aestheticizes, and in so doing, privatizes philosophy, for it holds it to be always merely speaking from the (contingent) preferences of its (contingent) author. One's theory cannot establish a relation to a real essence because there is nothing larger than oneself to incarnate. All vocabularies, including those responsible for making up the self, can always be replaced by being redescribed. And since nothing has a real essence, everything can be perspectivized (seen as making sense only within a particular narrative and hence subject to a different interpretation given a different context or narrative structure). In the words of Nancy Fraser, "every significant act would be an aesthetic act and every making a self-making."[4] Hence the call to be ironic, both about ourselves and about the point of human existence as well.

Like Nietzsche, Rorty revels in the doctrine of perspectivism. He valorizes the strong poet (Nietzsche's Übermensch) as one who is able to look perspectivism in the face and say "yes!" The strong poet is one who is able to create herself, to end her life knowing that the "final" vocabularies she has created are her own ("final vocabularies" are those sets of words which one chooses to use to justify one's actions and commitments, to formulate admiration and contempt, self-doubts and dreams). Thus Rorty presents us with a Romantic vision of the artist as an autonomous, idiosyncratic genius.

Herein lies the conflict between poetry and politics: the problem with this vision of artistic creation is that it is individualizing and elitist to the point where it demands a separation from all community. The strong poet exists in a sphere separate from (and even antithetical to) the demands and concerns of common life:

> The intellectual has a special idiosyncratic need—a need for the ineffable, the sublime, a need to go beyond the limits, a need to use words which are not part of anybody's language game, any social institutions. But one should not see the intellectual as serving a social purpose when he fulfills this need (HL 43).

On the one hand, then, one finds in Rorty this Romantic notion of the intellectual as being a thing apart, a notion which clearly devalues community or solidarity. But at the same time, one also finds in Rorty a pragmatic defense of bourgeois liberalism which clearly appeals to a notion of solidarity. The "institutions and practices of the rich North American democracies" are defended because they "work for us," because they foster economic, technological, and even moral, progress consistent with "our" needs. In lieu of any qualifications, this admittedly oversimplistic characterization of Rorty's defense of bourgeois liberalism contrasts with his notion of aestheticized culture in two important ways: first, his pragmatic notion of progress requires the opposite of artistic freedom—we must work in specific ways to achieve specific goals. This is antithetical to a vision which encourages us to perpetuate private idiosyncratic visions. Second, and related, it assumes a "we," a community who shares the same goals, needs, and desires. It necessitates a theory of solidarity foreign to the vision of the self-creating ironist. For example, history, in the ironist version, is simply a matter of redescription, a succession of a "mobile army of metaphors" (CIS 17) since "to change how we talk is to change how we are" (CIS 20). On the pragmatic political account, on the other hand, history would be seen, as Fraser notes, as a "succession of social problems posed and social problems solved, a succession that is in fact a progression" (Fraser 94). Instead of viewing progress privately as an aesthetic act of replacing old metaphors with new ones, it would be seen as having needed "common sense, technical competence and public-spiritedness" (Fraser 94), qualities foreign to the Romantic vision of the artist-intellectual.

These two impulses, the aesthetic and the political, each play a significant role in Rorty's recent writings. The problem is, however, that they seem to be at odds with one another. One way of stating the difference is that one is an essentially private, and hence non-political matter, the other an essentially public, and so political, one. Were Rorty to effect a happy reconciliation between the two, he would go a long way toward showing us how to reconcile what in Lyotard's work prevented a genuine politics of difference; namely, he would have reconciled paganism with politics and irony with solidarity.

In addressing this issue in Rorty's work I will present three different attempts at such reconciliation.[5] In the first, he views ironism and liberalism as, in the words of Fraser, "natural partners." In the second attempt he reverses himself and argues that they are in fact antithetical. In the third attempt he argues that they are neither natural partners nor antithetical to one another, but that one can effect a compromise by insisting on a separation between the public and private sectors. This allows one to be both a liberal and an ironist. This third position presumes to offer, finally, a notion of solidarity which permits the coexistence of the liberal with the ironist.

I shall argue that in the end the separation of the public and private spheres cannot be reconciled in the way Rorty wishes. But more important, I shall argue that Rorty's insistence on the distinction of the public from the private undermines the usefulness of his notion of community or solidarity because his public/private distinction lends itself to hierarchy and claims to sovereignty, and so does not allow for the fluidity of the public space which attention to difference demands. Finally, Rorty's surprising revitalization of a common human essence, revealed, he thinks, by our agreement that humiliation is the worst form of cruelty, makes his politics not simply misguided, but insidious.

The public utility of the ironists

Not only does Rorty argue that the ironist can peacefully coexist with the precepts of bourgeois liberalism, he further insists that the best ironist will also be a liberal. Since the ironist believes that the point of human life lies in the search for private perfection, she will value that negative freedom characteristic of liberal theory, a freedom whose function is to protect and allow for private vision. Indeed, Rorty claims that the very values of liberal society are the values that the poets and revolutionaries have handed down and the modus operandi suggested by the poet's uninvolvement in public affairs. Therefore liberal society ought to honor the strong poet as its founder and inspiration:

> . . . the heroes of liberal society are the strong poets and the utopian revolutionary. Such a synthesis will seem paradoxical if one thinks of the poet or revolutionary as necessarily "alienated from society" . . . But the paradox can be resolved. . . . An ideally liberal society is one in which whatever is both desirable and possible can be achieved by persuasion rather than force, reform rather than revolution, by the free and open encounters of present linguistic and other practices with suggestions for, and examples of, new practices. But this is to say that a liberal society is one which has no ideal except freedom, no goal except a willingness to see how such encounters go and to abide by the outcome. It is a *societas* rather than an *universitas* precisely because it has no purpose except to make life easier for poets and revolutionaries while seeing to it that they make life harder for others only by words, not by deeds [which is why

their separateness works to the advantage of the liberal society]. It is a society whose hero is the strong poet and the revolutionary because it recognizes that it is what it is, has the morality it has, speaks the language it does, not because it approximates the will of God, or the nature of man, but because certain poets and revolutionaries of the past spoke as they did (CC 13–14).

The liberal ironist has no desire for power, no wish to intrude on the public space, for she is properly ironic about her vision and influence. The ironist who is not bothered by the thought that her own redescriptions will be for her successors "just redescriptions" will not demand power; her attitude toward his successors will simply be "good luck to them" (CIS 102). The perfection the ironist sees is a private perfection, and she wishes only to be left in peace to peruse her self-creation, to write her "private poems" (CIS 20).

But the ironist does not simply write private poems in some secluded corner, having no effect on anyone but herself, wittingly or not, she also has public utility.

Rorty claims that there are "fairly tight connections between the freedom of the intellectuals on the one hand, and the diminution of cruelty on the other" (CC 14). To understand this we must recall his thesis that the human self is created by the use of vocabularies and that truths or criteria or facts are a property of language: "only descriptions of the world can be true or false" (CIS 5). This leads him to adopt a version of perspectivism: "anything could be made to look good or bad, important or unimportant, useful or useless, by being redescribed"; all is a matter of perspective. But then imagination becomes the all-important social tool, especially an imagination which is able to put into words what hasn't been put into words before, or which is unconstrained by the boundaries of the everyday. Such an imagination is the sole property of the strong poet, others are simply not raised to play the language game of critical reflection, and according to Rorty this makes the strong poet or ironist the most valuable social, cultural, and political commodity of liberal society.

Since what counts as cruel or unjust is "a matter of the language spoken," cruelties or injustices can only be overcome by instituting new forms of language. And here Rorty's Romantic vision of the ironist serves a social purpose. When conceived of as an idiosyncratic genius, existing outside the confines of the ordinary, the ironist is suited to be visionary, to invent new metaphors, in a way that no other member of society could be: "the strong poet is capable of telling the story of their own productions with words never used before" (CIS 11). The poet is therefore well suited to serve as the vanguard of the species: "Changing the way we talk changes what we want to do and what we think we are. The poet in the general sense of the maker of new words, the shaper of new languages, is the vanguard of the species" (CL 17).

Rorty argues that the non-ironist, and especially people who are oppressed by cruelty and suffering, are unable to engage in the language game of reflection or invention: "Victims of cruelty, people who are suffering do not have much in the way of language" (CIS 94), because pain makes them mute. Rorty argues that there can be no "voice of the oppressed" or "language of the victim" because the language once sufficient, and the only one these victims know and can imagine, is no longer working, and the victims are suffering too much to put new words into actions. Here again the ironist intellectual has an essential, social, and valuable, by liberal standards, role: the job of putting the situation of the victim into language is going to have to be done for them by someone else, and "the liberal novelist, poet, or journalist, is good at that" (CIS 94). The liberal novelist, poet, and journalist are skillful at imaginative identification. They are able to imagine a language for those who are unable to speak. Literature helps us to envision hitherto unspoken possibilities. It therefore not only makes change possible, it also enables change to take place consistent with liberal values: it makes us "kind" and "decent" by enabling us to be sensitive to and tolerant of other people's suffering (it presents the unpresentable). In this way solidarity is constructed out of little pieces. The ironist is the catalyst of liberalism.

Elitism and the dark side of liberal ironism

The identification of the ironist with the liberal gives us Rorty's first version of solidarity. Here poeticizing is linked with community-mindedness; to make society safe for the poets is to make it safe for everyone. Rorty has tried to present a convincing case for believing that aesthetic play and liberal reforms are really two sides of the same coin, that what promotes one will also promote the other, and that therefore "we" will all feel a loyalty to the liberal society which exists for the sake of promoting and protecting the values of the ironist.

These arguments, however, are not persuasive, first because the notion of "solidarity" does not allow for an account of difference, and second, because such arguments amount to a defense of elitism.

Consider the following:

> There are many objections to what I have been saying, but the one which I find most disturbing says that I am treating democratic societies as existing for the sake of intellectuals. I seem to be describing institutions which we constructed in order to prevent cruelty and obtain justice as if they had been constructed to safeguard the freedom of the leisured elite" (CC 14).

Indeed he has. And I cannot agree that such elitism is the price "all but a few eccentrics" would be willing to pay. The "few eccentrics" Rorty speaks of are in fact all those who are not part of the privileged elite.

Let me expand on the implications of his claim that non-intellectuals are not raised to play the language game necessary to critical reflection and imaginative identification. In making this claim, Rorty is both institutionalizing the specialness of the ironist intellectual and defending a society which promulgates the segregation and hegemony of language games. He writes: "In the ideal liberal society, the intellectuals would still be ironists, though non-intellectuals would not" (CIS 87). This statement is not just quaint, it is also dangerous, for it gives voice and the critical tool of reflection, the possibility of questioning and therefore of resistance or of bringing about change, only to the ironists. Of the rest he asserts,

> They would feel no more need to answer the question "*Why* are you liberal? Why do you care about the humiliation of strangers?" than the average sixteenth-century Christian felt to answer the question "why are you a Christian?" . . . (CIS 87).

"Such people are," he says, "not raised to play the language game in which one asks and gets justifications for that sort of belief" (CIS 87).

In passages such as these it becomes clear that the political arena, and laws in particular, is not simply necessary as a policing force guaranteeing negative freedoms. The distinction between the ironist intellectual and the non-reflective citizen is needed to ensure the distinctiveness of the ironist; marginalization, or the institutionalization of an Other, is necessary to guarantee the very possibility of ironism and the identity of the ironist self, for the ironist is essentially "reactive":

> I cannot . . . claim, that there could or ought to be a culture whose public rhetoric is *ironist*. I cannot imagine a culture which socialized its youth in such a way as to make them continuously dubious about their own process of socialization. . . . On my definition, an ironist cannot get along without the contrast between the final vocabularies she inherited and the one she is trying to create for herself. Ironists have to have something to have doubts about, something from which to be alienated (CIS 87).

The Other which serves the ironist best is liberal society: "The ironist is the typical modern intellectual [*sic*!], and the only society which gives her freedom to articulate her alienation are liberal ones" (CIS 89).

The distinction between the ironist intellectual and the non-intellectual serves then as a means of oppression. And I find this very dangerous indeed. If the means to recognize the source of the beliefs one holds are institutionally placed beyond the reach of, or kept from, the majority of the population, then so too is the possibility of questioning and therefore of resistance. The chances of meaningful resistance are further limited because while Rorty's ideal is that doubts about the public rhetoric of the culture are only legitimate where they can be met with "concrete alternatives and programs," he would have society structured in such a way as to have already limited the imaginative capabilities of the non-ironists, thereby ensuring the institutionalization of ignorance or submissiveness. To anticipate my discussion of Foucault, Rorty aids in the construction of the domination of normalizing and disciplinary regimes.

We have seen that the privileging of the intellectual artist is further justified on the ground that they are the voice of the oppressed, and so the voice of kindness and decency, our window to tolerance and sensitivity. Rorty believes it makes sense to order our society to benefit the strong poets because it benefits all of us to protect that class of people not silenced by pain and suffering; only the poets can free the rest of us to be genuinely human.

Rorty claims to be "torn between insisting that the welfare of the dissident poets ought to be of interest to the non-poets, and wondering whether we say this simply because we ourselves find it easier to identify with poets than with peasants" (CC 14). I suggest that the very terms in which this dilemma is posed make the answer clear: better a poet than a peasant. And if the two are so far apart, why should we be comfortable believing that the poet's version of oppression, cruelty, pain, and suffering really speak to the experience of the victims? And who is this "we," anyway?

Is the poet really able to get outside of her own situation to understand that of another as she would have herself understood? We cannot be sanguine about the suggestion that there is no voice of the oppressed or about the consequence that the leisured elite will speak for them. (Which is not to suggest that the oppressed speak with a single voice, but only that they do speak! And that the voice of the intellectual is not the only voice.) This is simply wishful speaking on the part of one who is already satisfied with his position as a beneficiary of rich North American democracies. But what if one is not so satisfied?

Rorty offers a weak defense of liberal society not only because those silenced by pain and those genius ironists are two extremes between which lie the majority of the people. Even if we agree that society's primary commitment should be to those most in pain, one would still wonder why we should believe that the privileged novelist or poet will see the world from a standpoint commensurable with those who are institutionally marginalized. We would do well to question how, to what extent, or even whether the artist is able to escape the hegemony of culture. In fact, a valuable contribution of aesthetic critique to politics—given the fact that from the standpoint of those in marginalized positions, the oppressed are in fact speaking for themselves—has been precisely to point out the ideological component of representation: the artist's depiction of the laborer, or woman, or people of color, or the aging have all too often served to reinforce that kind of seeing which strengthens the ideological grip of the status quo.[6] So long as the Romantic view is the ideal, the cultural images which proliferate will be consistent with the dominance of patriarchal power. In placing the artists beyond the understanding of the common folk, Romanticism places such images beyond the ken of critical reflection. The Romantic vision of the artist is thus political: it serves to assure the continuance of the status quo. And in representing this voice as the voice of all its citizens, the "solidarity" it engenders is indeed terroristic.

Rorty's view being presented in this section, namely that Romanticism and liberalism are easy bedfellows, is also defended by his claim that ironism or aesthetic play will not only be consistent with, but will promote, liberal values such as kindness, decency, tolerance, and a loathing of cruelty. He believes this is consistent with his view that humiliation is the worst form of cruelty we can effect on one another (which will be a claim I will call into question). Indeed, some private poems might be consistent with these ideals. But will all? Here my worry is that far from being a knight of liberal values and social hope, the true fact of the matter is that the ironist and the aestheticized society is antithetical to just those things. This is because as Rorty presents them, the task of the strong poet is the "devaluation of values," and this is, in fact, inimical to his erstwhile defense of liberalism.

This paradox leads me to consider another formulation of the relation between the ironist and the liberal—or between aesthetics and the private, which the ironist stands for, and the political and the public, which is the exclusive property of the liberal domain.

Ironist as antichrist

> When one has grasped that the "subject" is not something
> that creates effects, but only a fiction, much follows.
> (Nietzsche, *The Will To Power*.)

It turns out that the ironist is particularly ill suited to serve as the social messiah.

What makes the strong poet strong is the same thing that serves to make her reactive; she is ironic about there being any goal beyond that of fashioning her private self-image. And that image may be fashioned in any way she chooses—she is not constrained by normative sanctions. Her only concern is with the search for novelty: novel experiences and novel languages. This exemplifies Rorty's ideal of the best life possible for him, if not for anyone, to lead: "the perfect life will be one which closes in the assurance that the last of his final vocabularies, at least, were wholly his" (CIS 9).

Rorty is clear that this entails the claim that even events which exemplify "extreme cruelty" are simple private poems, and as such, must be seen as continuous with any other activity. Calling something cruel is simply "one more redescription to be filed alongside all the others," "one more vocabulary," "one more set of metaphors."

This "ironic" attitude is surely one we would not want our policymakers to adopt. While the ironist may be a suitable hero to the poet, she is not a suitable role model for the "ideal citizen."

There is the following to be considered: since the poets are precisely those people who do not talk as we do, they will necessarily appear, from the vantage of the ordinary citizen, to be "irrational and immoral" (CC 14). The ironist is moved by the call 'change for change's sake!'; this is the substance of her freedom. But the non-ironist will not be so moved. She will want to be convinced that the change is *preferable*. And what reason could there be to think the ironist's regime would make her better off—especially since, from her perspective, such a regime will foster unreason and immorality? Given the fact that from the point of view of the masses, the language of the ironist will necessarily be seen as irrational and immoral, it would be unreasonable for the non-ironist to allow the ironist to be the vanguard of social hope; in fact it would be masochistic.

In his defense of elitism, in his attempt at reconciling liberalism and ironism, Rorty has argued that "we must side with the Romantics and do our best to aestheticize society, to keep it safe for the poets in the hope that the poets may eventually make it safe for everybody else" (CIS 61). But he also recognizes the danger of this: "The attempts of leftist intellectuals to pretend that the avant-garde is serving the wretched of the earth . . . is a hopeless attempt to make the special needs of the intellectual and the social needs of the community coincide. Such an attempt goes back to the Romantic period" (HL 43), a period he here reviles.

In fact, Rorty worries that the coincidence of irony and theory, poetry and public policy, has devastating public effects. This is the substance of his charge against the theoretical ironist.

Nietzsche, Hegel, and Heidegger are all "ironist theorists" rather than "ironist liberals" because they cling to a desire for power and impinge on the public space (they are, to use Lyotard's term, "unpure"). They are neglectful of the fact that their theories are only private poems and cannot have any theoretical significance—we may choose to adopt some part of their "poem" for our own self-image, but we cannot be told to do so. So long as Nietzsche and Heidegger stick to celebrating their personal canons, Rorty claims they are magnificent. They are, he argues, "figures whom the rest of us can use as material in our own attempts to create a new self by writing a *Bildungsroman* about our old self" (CIS 119). They become problematic, however, as soon as they overstep the boundary between theory and politics and take themselves to be doing something more than writing private poems: "as soon as either tries to put forward a view about modern society, or the destiny of Europe, or contemporary politics, they become at best vapid, and at worst sadistic" (CIS 120).

Rorty's claim is that this is not accidental, rather it is illustrative of the fact that irony has little public use:

> Metaphysics hoped to bring together our private and our public lives by showing us that self-discovery and political utility could be united. It hoped to provide a final vocabulary which would not break apart into a private and a public portion. It hoped to be both beautiful on a small scale and sublime on a large public one. Ironist theory ran its course in the attempt to achieve this same synthesis through narrative rather than system. But the attempt was hopeless (CIS 120).

He insists that:

> "[i]ronists should reconcile themselves to a private-public split within their final vocabularies. . . . Colligation and redescription of the little things that are important to one—even if those little things are philosophy books—will not result in an understanding of anything larger than oneself, anything like "Europe" or "History." We should stop trying to combine self-creation and politics especially if we are liberals (CIS 120).

There is a normative worry underlying his claim that self-creation and politics must be kept distinct. As judged from the perspective of liberal values, ironists can be cruel.

In a reversal of the picture of the ironist as one who is concerned to engender empathetic understanding, and respect the values of kindness, tolerance, and sensitivity, we are reminded of the delight, coincident with perspectivism, of redescription: "Ironism, as I have defined it, results from awareness of the power of redescription." But redescription does not lend itself to the liberal's recommendation for social practice:

> Most people do not want to be redescribed. They want to be taken on their own terms—taken seriously just as they are and just as they talk. The ironist tells them that the language they speak is up for grabs by her and her kind. There is something potentially very cruel about that claim. For the best way to cause people long-lasting pain is to humiliate them by making the things that seem most important to them look futile, obsolete, and powerless . . . redescription often humiliates (CIS 89–90).

But this leads to a reversal of what was stated in the last section. It now seems that the ironist is particularly ill suited to serve in the vanguard of liberal democracy. From the standpoint of the non-intellectual she will be arrogant, heartless, and cruel. From the standpoint of the ironist, the least desirable thing will be to be identified with a unified, conservative, civilized society:

> On my definition, an ironist cannot get along without the contrast between the final vocabulary she inherited and the one she is trying to create for herself. Irony is, if not intrinsically resentful, at least reactive. Ironists have to have something to have doubts about, something from which to be alienated (CIS 88).

Thus Rorty presents us with the "dark side" of ironism, and in so doing, would appear to have given us no choice between the aestheticized society and the liberal one, between ironism and pragmatism, individualism or solidarity, poetry or politics, the private or the public. There seems to be no way to split the difference.

And yet he denies that these dichotomies represent incompatibilities. Rorty insists that it must be possible for a single society to accommodate the goals of liberalism and the values of the ironist for a single person to be both an ironist and a liberal; in fact, this is the impetus for his current writings. The question is, how is this possible and at what price are such reconciliations bought?

The public-private split: bifurcating the beast

Rorty's rueful conclusion in response to the difficulties the dark side of ironism presents to the well-working of a liberal polity is to say that he has been mistaken in his attempts to unite them: "We must stop trying to unite decency and sublimity." The fact of the matter is, "irony has little public use" (CIS 120).

And so he insists on a bifurcation between the public and the private dimension of both our individual lives, and the culture at large. The private is the realm of the ironist, the public the realm of politics.

What is at stake in the division is the following: intellectual disciplines, metaphysics, philosophy, theory—as well as aesthetic impulses to creativity and innovation—are aligned under the auspices of the private. This is kept distinct from pragmatic concerns, social policy, and instrumental rationality, all of which are the sole concerns of the public sphere (PDP 272). On the one hand we have the makings for autonomy, on the other, for solidarity. The private is equated with a concern for the self, with private happiness and perfection, the public with a concern for group welfare and social utility.

Theory and practice must be kept distinct. Only then can they peacefully coexist. This means that there can be no philosophers of public life; the sole use of ironist theory is private: to aid in the novel creation of self-images. As Fraser aptly notes, this puts the role of the intellectual in a very different light from the one previously described. He cannot be the vanguard of social hope:

> Clearly, the partisan position entails a revised view of the social role and political function of the intellectual. The strong poet as heretofore conceived must be domesticated, cut down to size and made fit for private life. . . . The intellectual will be king in the castle of his own self-fashioning, but he will no longer legislate for the social world. Indeed, the intellectual will have no social role or political function (Fraser 101).

Pragmatism and instrumental rationality rule in the public sphere. For this philosophers are not needed: "Politics can be separated from beliefs about matters of ultimate importance" (PDP 257). Such beliefs are irrelevant to the social order, though they may be relevant, or even essential, to individual perfection: "Colligation and redescription of the little things that are important to one—even if those little things are philosophy books—will not result in an understanding of anything larger than oneself . . ." (CIS 120).

This splitting of the public and the private is Rorty's best attempt to find a way to achieve his goal of allowing for a person who is both a liberal and an ironist, a culture which is both liberal and poeticized. Indeed, as he says, the success of his theory stands or falls with the success of his public/private distinction (CIS 83).

But in that case we are forced to conclude that he fails. He fails on his own terms; in fact he is not able to keep his liberalism from intruding on what should be the private sphere—his liberalism is theoretical. But then theory, which properly belongs to the private/aesthetic sphere, is intruding on the public/political sphere, intruding, in other words, where it doesn't belong. He also fails in the terms of a postmodern politics or a politics of difference which cannot accept the political consequences of drawing such distinctions. This should be objectionable to Rorty as well, for it forces him to renege on that which motivates his ironism, namely, the thesis that language, the self, and community are all a function of a human, and thus a cultural and social, vocabulary.

This self, the self consistent with the contingency thesis, is seen as being necessarily constituted in a world of others. As Richard King correctly notes, "There is no 'one' without 'two' or more, and so our private concerns and judgement have social origins and implications."[7] Thus, the process of attempting to construct our own self-images will reveal the fact that we are always already social beings: the "building blocks of our narratives—our experiences, actions, values, sense of the world and its possibilities—are derived from the social world (which is itself also a construct). Our narrated/narrating self, which is never fixed or defined once and for all, has social foundations."[8] This is to say that if we agree to the poststructuralist theory of the self and language—a theory which, I would argue, is politically useful even if it cannot be metaphysically defined—then we must also agree to the thesis that the private sphere and the cultural sphere which include the "private" cannot be delineated. Both the private and the public are political constructs.

Rorty's blindness to this point is evidence of his (ironism notwithstanding) entrenchment in the Anglo-American tradition, which is staunchly individualist. It sees the self as being fully human only to the extent that he or she is a participant in the public realm, but the presupposition of that participation is the independent and autonomous citizen. This notion of autonomy is a holdover from the modernist tradition, which should have been repudiated by the poststructuralist/ironist theorist. Rorty's assumption that there is a private self which can be formulated *independently* of the public one neglects the social origins and implications of the self.

It also neglects the political dimensions of the self, since, I would argue, that thesis which insists that the self is culturally or socially constructed cannot ignore the fact that the cultural and the social are themselves constructed within the stakes of power. This is not just Foucault's insight, it is also the lesson of the social movements of the last century. Again, Nancy Fraser puts this point well:

> Workers' movements, for example, especially as clarified by Marxist theory, have taught us that the economic is political. Likewise, women's movements, as illuminated by feminist theory, have taught us that the domestic and the personal are political [I would add, that this insight also comes to us through proponents of gay and

lesbian rights]. Finally, a whole range of New Left social movements, as illuminated by Gramscian, Foucauldian, and yes, even by Althusserian theory, have taught us that the cultural, the medical, the educational—everything that Hannah Arendt called "the social," as distinct from the private and the public—that all this too is political (Fraser 102).

Yet, she argues, and I concur, Rorty's "partisan position" "requires us to bury these insights, to turn our backs on the last hundred years." Classical liberalism, which Rorty speaks for, refuses to see those actions it considers private as being power-laden, political. In other words, such voices as those of the New Left speak to the uselessness—and indeed from the standpoint of difference, to the danger of classical liberalism. Moreover, Fraser notes that the theory of solidarity coincident with classical liberalism assumes the hegemony of social space. Rorty assumes that there will

> . . . be no deep social cleavages capable of generating conflicting solidarities and opposing "we's." It follows from this assumed absence of fundamental social antagonisms that politics is a matter of everyone pulling together to solve a common set of problems. Thus social engineering can replace political struggle. Disconnected tinkerings with a succession of allegedly discrete social problems can replace transformation of the basic institutional structure (Fraser 104).

Such a notion of solidarity depoliticizes the concerns of anyone who speaks with a voice other than that of the bourgeois liberal. In aligning theory on the side of the private, concerns with collective life on the side of the public, and keeping in mind that the ironist, whose realm is the private, is cast as the reactive, Romantic hero, Rorty's partisan position ensures the political impotence of radical discourse and the political dominance of the bourgeois liberal. It makes non-liberal, oppositional discourses

> non-political by definition . . . Political discourse in fact is restricted by Rorty to those who speak the language of bourgeois liberalism. Whatever departs from that vocabulary simply lacks any sense of solidarity. . . . The adherents of bourgeois liberalism have a monopoly on talk about community needs and social problems. Whoever eschews the liberal idiom must be talking about something else—about, say, individual salvation (Fraser 102–5).

The point is that those interactions which classical liberalism considers private are power-laden and political, and the "solidarity" which Rorty's bourgeois liberalism assumes to be theory neutral is in fact theory laden—it speaks for a particular class- and gender-biased perspective.

Rorty's partisan position, which is his last word on the reconciliation of pluralism with politics, is glaringly ill suited to serve the goal of demarginalization. Demarginalizing those whose concerns are other than the capitalist bourgeois liberal's is coincident with politicizing those voices who have been institutionally kept within the sphere of the private, either through their class, sex, sexual preference, or education. Rorty poeticizes what needs to be politicized.

Freeing the "private" from the private, making it susceptible to political critique, public-critical reflection (an oxymoron on Rorty's terms) and political debate, thereby making the larger society amenable to change in directions which accommodate the demand of those who feel themselves institutionally marginalized, is one necessary step in the formation of oppositional politics. A theory like Rorty's, which institutionalizes the public/private split, institutionalizes marginalization and therefore oppression. Consensus which is formed within a public sphere distinct from the "private" is indeed terroristic.

This point could also be put in Fraser's terms: in confining his notion of solidarity to the collective concerns of the bourgeois liberal, Rorty gives us "no possibility for a genuinely radical political discourse rooted in oppositional solidarities;" but an adequate notion of politics must be able to accommodate "radical discourse *communities*" that contest dominant discourses (Fraser 105). I would add, it must also be able to distinguish dominant from subordinate solidarities; totality must not be universalized. Rorty's partisan position neither engenders solidari*ties*, nor can it offer a critique of power (much less a critical reflection on its own power biases).

The fact that Rorty is not able to view the public and the private as being distinctions institutionalized for the purposes of hegemonic regimes shows that he is unable to combine politics with pluralism and is evidence of one more failure of the attempt at a genuine instantiation of postmodern politics. I agree that giving up the vocabulary in which worries about relativism make sense is a necessary step in achieving such a goal. But equally necessary is the removal of any attempt to bifurcate the public and the private—indeed, insisting on the ubiquity of the political is crucial in achieving a postmodern and oppositional politics.

Universalizing totality: cultural imperialism and the hegemony of the Rortian liberal

> On my view, we should be more willing than we are to celebrate bourgeois capitalist society as the best polity actualized so far, while regretting that it is irrelevant to most of the problems of most of the population of the planet. (Rorty, *On the Consequences of Pragmatism.*)

> What do you consider most humane?—To spare someone shame. (Nietzsche, *The Gay Science*)

Distinguishing the public from the private is of central political importance for Rorty because he says it inculcates reflective doubt: keeping the distinction before us will cause us to have self-doubts about our sensitivity to the pain and humiliation of others. We will recognize the need to distinguish the question "Do you believe and desire what I believe and desire?" from the question "Are you suffering?" Rorty says, "In my jargon, this is the ability to distinguish the question of whether you and I share the same final vocabulary from the question of whether you are in pain." Distinguishing these questions makes it possible to distinguish public from private questions, questions about pain from questions about the point of human life, the domain of the liberal from the domain of the ironist. It thus makes it "possible for a single person to be both" (CIS 197), and this he takes to be his crowning achievement. In the last section I have shown how his crown, even if earned, is tarnished. We should not *want* a theory which necessitates the separation of private from public questions.

In this section I will argue that the crown is not only tarnished, but is also not earned; in fact Rorty is not able to maintain the separation of his liberal/political from his ironic/private concerns. In the wedding of liberalism and ironism, one of the partners is dominated by the other—such a marriage does violence to ironism.

I need to take the time here to make clear what is at stake in the survival of ironism for the purposes of my larger project, for the project is not simply to criticize Rorty, but to see whether there is something here I can borrow to bolster the claim that the radical pluralism of a postmodern politics is necessary at the same time as oppositional politics must also admit the necessity of similarity *and* difference.

Whatever difficulties the particulars of Rorty's ironism, as with Lyotard's paganism, may present, it nevertheless contains the expression of radical pluralism. Crucial to all sufficiently radical pluralisms on my understanding is the thesis of perspectivism, difference, and play. This is what I am trying to combine with an oppositional politics. But I argued in the last section, such a politics claims that the tools from which we build our self-images are *social, cultural* tools, and hence that our self-images and identities—even if they are multiple and sometimes fragmented—are social/cultural identities. Rorty does not see this. He argues that "vocabularies are tools rather than mirrors," but he is mistaken; they are tools *and* they are mirrors. Therefore, a politics that addresses the oppression of these kinds of subjects will have to do it socially (publicly). Insofar as it instantiates the Romantic vision of the idiosyncratic genius, Rorty's ironism is unacceptable. We can never exist "alone" in his sense. What is at stake in the following then is not simply whether or not Rorty's ironism survives his liberalism, but whether radical pluralism survives his politics. If it cannot, then he cannot serve us as a model for oppositional politics.

The charge that his ironism does not survive his liberal politics can be substantiated in more than one way. First, Rorty is guilty of a contradiction when he claims that ironism is subordinate to the demands of liberalism, for he also gives the demands of liberalism moral priority: he demands that in such cases where one's private projects conflict with the public good (the public good being determined by whatever serves best to minimize the possibility of humiliation), these projects must be privatized. This request for privatizing, he says, "amounts to the request that they resolve an impending dilemma by subordinating sublimity to the desire to avoid cruelty and pain" (CIS 197).

Here we see that political danger is avoided, but at too high a cost—it is avoided by subordinating the demands of the ironist to the demands of the liberal, and if this is the case then he has failed in his project: he has not combined liberalism and ironism in one person—rather he describes a liberal who has an ironic side to his nature which is allowed free rein when suitable. And indeed, as he feared, we have here an example of the danger of combining ironism and social action. Rorty uses the cruelty made possible by his superior ironic talents in the pursuit of his liberal ideals:

> If one's moral identity consists in being a citizen of a liberal polity, then to encourage light-mindedness will serve one's moral purposes. Moral commitment, after all, does not require taking seriously all the matters that are, for moral reasons, taken seriously by one's fellow citizens. It may require just the opposite. It may require trying

to josh them out of the habit of taking those topics so seriously . . .
(PDP 272).

The "joshing" being recommended here as a useful, in fact *necessary*
strategy for "moral progress" sounds like another word for humiliation; Rorty has no qualms about being cruel when the stakes are
changing the ideas of those who are a threat to the liberal version of
progress. Here we see instantiated the terror of technocratic rationality
so loathed by Lyotard. Be that as it may, liberal values will out.
In cases where the freedoms granted the ironist conflict with liberal
institutions, it is clear that Rorty feels the public is justified in subduing
the private.

Another way in which my charge can be supported is to point out
that the constraints liberalism places on self-creation amount to a form
of cultural imperialism, and this can be argued in a number of ways.
I propose to iterate some of these arguments in the following pages.

(a) It is only his naive faith in liberal values which allows him to
remain sanguine about the unacceptable political repercussions of his
ethnocentrism.

Rorty has no qualms about admitting that this commitment to liberalism is a reflection of his ethnocentrism:

> There is no *neutral*, non-circular, way to defend the liberal's claim
> that cruelty [I assume that by this he means humiliation] is the
> worst thing we do, anymore that there is a neutral way to back up
> Nietzsche's claim that this expresses a resentful, slavish, attitude.
> . . . We cannot look back behind the process of socialization which
> convinced us twentieth-century liberals of this claim and appeal to
> something more real . . . *we* have to start from where *we* are . . .
> that is part of the force of Sellar's claim that we are under no
> obligations other than the "we" intentions of the communities with
> which we identify (CIS 197).

And in another chapter he argues that the ironist's ability to envisage
the desire to prevent the actual and possible humiliation of others
"despite differences of sex, race, tribe, and final vocabularies" is, he
assures us, "not associated with any larger power than that embodied
in a concrete historical situation, e.g., the power of the rich European
and American democracies to disseminate their customs to other parts
of the world" (CIS 93). So ironists *ought* to be liberal.

Rorty feels that the dissemination of rich European and American
culture amounts to "moral progress." But in all of this his liberal

ideals cannot mask its endemic hegemony—a form of oppression which moreover does not even take into account the diversity or plurality of its *own* culture. Rorty seems impervious to the fact that the people living in European or American democracies are not all rich, not all liberal, and do not even necessarily feel themselves to be given genuine democratic options. The "we" Rorty speaks to is much smaller than he imagines—and it is just this fact which makes his liberalism and the subordination of the private pluralist projects to public liberal goals so unacceptable to those searching for a politics of difference. It may also indicate the limit of his philosophical interest for those of us who do not buy into his biases for he seems to be speaking only to those who, like himself, are predisposed toward the ideals of bourgeois liberalism.

(b) Far from creating a larger and more variegated ethos, moral progress which conceives of itself as moving in the direction of human solidarity—*where "solidarity" has not been redescribed to fit the demands of pluralism and so necessarily excludes difference*—cannot help but do violence to pluralist commitments, cannot help but construct unacceptable metaphysical foundations to justify itself. Rorty thinks that his notion of moral progress and solidarity is unproblematic because despite the differences among final vocabularies, he believes that there will be enough overlap in words such as *decency, kindness,* and *dignity* to make the recognition of pain in others possible—enough overlap, in other words, to allow "imaginative identification" (CIS 93).

> Solidarity is not thought of as recognition of a core self, the human essence in all human beings", but rather "thought of as the ability to see more and more traditional differences (of tribe, religion, race, customs and the like) as unimportant when compared with their similarity in respect to pain and humiliation—the ability to think of people wildly different from oneself as included in the range of "us" (CIS 192).

But the radical pluralism which follows upon his ironism ought to force Rorty to recognize that any solidarity which is conceived of as an absence of difference is invalid according to the precepts of pluralism: there is no "us"—in the sense of something which forms a core identity to which conflict is absent, a core which is static and unchanging—ranging over difference. But I find such a recognition to be missing. Despite his insistence that his notion of solidarity is non-metaphysical, it nevertheless cannot make sense without his understanding of a common human essence (and here I am reminded of Lyotard's need for a Justice beyond justice): the core of each self reveals a "moral subject," e.g., "something which can be humiliated" (CIS 91). Such a notion of moral progress is ahistorical, and so violates one of the central canons of pluralism.

(c) Rorty fails to see that his very choice of the worst kind of pain, humiliation, betrays his inability to affect an unconcern with public appearances suited to the strong poet (he fails to be ironic), and assumes the modernist notion of subjectivity which presupposes that there are essences underlying difference. It is also indicative of the retention of highly questionable values, among which is non-ironic machoism.

Of all pains, humiliation is in particular peculiar for an ironist to single out, for it is a pain which evinces a failure to be properly ironic about self-description. One can be humiliated only if one has a stake in, or values, a particular description of oneself—only if one is holding on to an essentialist notion of the self. The ironist, however, who values protean change above all ought to look forward to having new descriptions of himself shown to him as possible tools of self-creation. Far from being a cause of humiliation, the intrusion of contrary self-descriptions would keep the ironist honest.

Furthermore, while we may not have conscious recourse to all the cultural beliefs which ignite the pain of humiliation, surely this, perhaps even more so than other pains such as hunger, is a cultural construct masking the biases of the dominant powers. In the modern, Western tradition, for example, humiliation is the name of a pain which is tied up with the macho values of competition, glory and heroism, and the macho fear of cowardice—tied up, in other words, with the tradition of bourgeois liberalism.

So we see that even that supposedly natural category which legitimates solidarity is itself informed by the liberal individualist and patriarchal worldview, a view which does not speak for humanity as such.

(d) Even if one does not agree with my depiction of humiliation as speaking to particularly macho values, Rorty's use of it remains problematic. Rorty wants to say that fear of humiliation gives us the overlap necessary to speak a common language, but as soon as humiliation is given anything more than a merely formal content, the absurdity of this suggestion becomes evident. The "traditional" differences of tribe, religion, race, customs, and the like cannot, as Rorty claims it can, be separated out of the material definition of pain and humiliation. In this as in all else, the pervasiveness of politics and acculturation goes all the way down. Humiliation is a material, not a formal concept, and once the plurality of the material definition of humility is recognized, its inadequacy to serve as that which unites humans in solidarity is evident.

(e) Rorty says he wants to promote "a story of increasing willingness to live with plurality and stop asking for universal validity" (CIS 67), but his notion of moral progress and solidarity demands the assimilation of otherness. He believes that the detailed descriptions of particular varieties of pain and humiliation described for us by the novelist or ethnographer are the modern intellectual's principal contribution to moral progress (CIS 192). And yet, from an ironist's perspective, the failure of an author must be measured precisely by the extent to which the Other has been made amenable to assimilation of an "us." There is no reason to feel easy either in the novelist's or the ethnographer's ability to transcend his or her own language, nor is there any reason to believe that translating from one culture to another will not do damage to the *Sinn* of otherness.

Rorty claims that what counts as cruelty or injustice is a matter of the language spoken. But then it would seem that we cannot help speaking of otherness in our own terms, and this necessarily does violence to that otherness. This seems inevitable unless there is one language we all speak. But such essentialism is denied the ironist. In summary, the fact that Rorty's liberalism is ethnocentric, that it harbors unacceptable metaphysical foundations, that humiliation is an example of such a bias and is also ethnocentric and does not speak to a common human pain, that humiliation is, furthermore, a material and not a formal concept, and finally that the language of the novelist or ethnographer does not speak for or to a common human experience, are all evidence of my claim that the constraints Rorty's liberalism places on self-creation amount to a form of cultural imperialism.

To conclude: universal concepts, be they morality, rationality, subjectivity, decency, or humiliation, have force only so long as what marks us out as being the individuals we are is ignored. And they are all, I would argue, politically dangerous concepts in that their supposed neutrality always masks a particular, non-universal, political agenda. This is clear in the case of Rorty, who blithely defends the institutions of Western democracies, even if they entail oppression, on the ground that such institutions lessen cruelty and suffering. This is, I claim, a naive view. Whether or not it lessens cruelty and suffering is a matter of how those terms are conceived, and if ironism and postmodern politics has anything to teach us it is the infinite variety of such narrative constructions.

Rorty reconsidered

None of Rorty's three positions presents an adequate solution to the reconciliation of aesthetics and politics. Rorty does not unite irony with a sufficiently postmodern notion of solidarity and so his form of "consensus" does indeed legitimate Lyotard's concern regarding terror.

The first position makes the ironist intellectual the spokesperson of the non-ironist, non-intellectual. The good of the ironist is also what is good for society, therefore it is acceptable to construct democratic institutions to safeguard the freedom of the leisured elite (CC 14). I have argued the unacceptability of this position; elitism is too high a price to pay for solidarity, for the "solidarity" is not only betrayed by its being synonymous with the leisured white bourgeois male liberal, it is also instantiated in such a way as to ensure that it is immune to critique from discordant voices. This notion of solidarity leaves no room for oppositional politics—it universalizes totality.

The second position fails because it casts ironism as antithetical to solidarity and politics—it universalizes difference. The ironist is construed as essentially reactive. But as Nancy Fraser points out, this has the consequence that all radical theorizing has the status of a private poem and this is unacceptable politically, for "not all radical theorizing is elitist, antidemocratic, and opposed to collective concerns and political life" (Fraser 102).

Furthermore, I would add that this position denies that solidarity can be based on critical reflection, since critical reflection is the sole property of the ironist. But then the "solidarity" Rorty is presenting us with is unacceptable, for in denying the non-intellectual the possibility of critical reflection, it denies oppositional politics, one of whose goals is creating the conditions under which marginalized groups can form their own identities, its most essential tool.

Lastly, I have also argued that the Romantic portrayal of the ironist as reactionary and alone, betrays one of the most important insights of poststructuralism and postmodernism: while Rorty's position of the ironist is consistent with the claim that we create ourselves out of the tools of language, it fails to note the cultural and social constraints of language; vocabularies are not simply tools, they are also mirrors.[9]

The third position fails because the public cannot be kept distinct from the private. This is related to my insistence on the acculturation of language—if our options for self-creation are given to us by a cultural vocabulary (there are no private languages), then, borrowing from Foucault, all knowledge is a form of power. This is demonstrated by my suggestion that even when he is theorizing the public/private split, Rorty is not able to maintain the division—his conception of the private is informed throughout by his political (and partisan) biases. So too is the notion of solidarity that unites the public and the private, "making it possible for a single person to be both: a liberal and an ironist." Finally, and I think importantly, humiliation which forms the basis of such solidarity is a macho form of suffering, and at any rate is certainly not the worst form of cruelty "we" can experience.

3

Foucault

I would like to begin this chapter by recalling the discussion of poststructuralism that began the chapter on Lyotard. In that discussion I claimed that Lyotard's aesthetic and political commitment to unconstrained discourse and self-constructions gets its impetus from the Derridian notion of play and difference. Since he accepts the model of the self as an endlessly differed system of signs, he sees any closure as excluding some other, equally valid, description of the self. This thesis becomes politicized in his notion of terror: any imposition of a discourse—be it a set of juridical rules, a scientist notion of rationality, an essentialist notion of human nature, or whatever—forces conformity to a norm, and in so doing, is silencing the multiplicity that is the "actual" mark of the self.

In Lyotard, the politicizing of the themes of poststructuralism—his concern for the Other—are carried on within a postmodern politics: Lyotard attempts to give voice to the Other by denying the legitimacy of grand narratives. His task can be alternatively described as demarginalizing marginalized voices (presenting the unpresentable) or as marginalizing the dominant voices (refusing to privilege any particular viewpoint). The former corresponds to his search for the Justice of multiplicity, the latter to his insistence that justice be understood as multiplicity.

I have argued that Lyotard fails in his attempt to politicize his poststructuralist commitments: he fails to offer a viable politics both because his impulse to universalize difference makes impossible any kind of consensus or notion of community, and because in universalizing unity in his discussion of terror he fails to be able to distinguish terroristic from non-terroristic forms of consensus, unity, or community.

As with Lyotard, Rorty is also committed to the deconstructive themes of poststructuralism, though he forgets this when it suits him to do so. As we have seen, his politicizing of the themes of poststructuralism shows itself in his concern to organize the political space in such a way as to guarantee the freedom of the strong poets, and his politicizing of the themes of postmodernism presents itself in his ironic eschewal of grand narratives. Like Lyotard, he presumes to be committed to giving a voice to the marginalized Other, though unlike Lyotard, this concern bespeaks a kind of elitism; it is not the voice of the marginalized Other as oppressed minorities that occupies Rorty, but that of the intellectual, of the strong poet. In the end, the voice he wants to promote is not that of the Other, but that of the colonizer.

That this makes Rorty's brand of poststructuralism unsuitable for the concerns of oppositional politics is evident from his understanding of the nature of aesthetics, which is to a large degree what informs the felt need for the public/private split. The poststructural description of language along with its insistence on the play of signification informs Rorty's perspectivism. He sees the self as always being open to redescription and so as being a work of art. With this in mind he describes the best functioning human being as one who constructs her or his life out of her or his own narratives. But here Rorty has ignored a fundamental tenet of poststructuralism, i.e., that the tools of self-construction are always culturally inscribed—vocabularies are mirrors as well as tools—and that therefore, the self is never its own construction if by such a construction one has in mind the Romantic notion of the idiosyncratic genius whose creation is freed from the exigencies of the everyday. Such a view of artworks overlooks a fundamental political fact, a fact consistent with the demands of poststructuralism: insofar as it is a carrier of cultural signification (and is itself a cultural signifier) artworks always have a political component, though the political signification of an artwork may be more or less immediate and important.

This understanding of the artwork is significant for our understanding of the subject, for the subject is understood by Rorty as being itself a work of art. Rorty's bracketing of the implications of his commitment to the poststructuralist understanding of the cultural embeddedness of signs for his understanding of the self-as-artwork has serious consequences for the political acceptability of his understanding of the public and the private. It undermines the viability of his understanding of the public because the public for Rorty is synonymous with the social, the scientific, and the juridical norms of bourgeois liberalism. Rorty ignores the limited perspective of the "we" encompassed by bourgeois liberalism, and so, his understanding of the public forecloses on alternative challenges to the norms of bourgeois liberalism because it assumes that the norms of his preferred public speak for "the good of man." His cavalier acknowledgment, when pressed, that this is ethnocentric and amounts to no more than a cultural bias (and a gendered and economic and class bias) does nothing to lessen the consequences, invalid from the standpoint of his erstwhile poststructuralist commitment to difference, of such a view. This criticism is especially telling from a political perspective because his "pragmatic" defense of his ethnocentrism amounts to the statement, "This works according to the criteria of my viewpoint and after all, this is the only viewpoint I can be expected to have," and, "If the politics of bourgeois capitalist society is irrelevant to most of the problems of most of the population of the planet, well, those problems which are irrelevant to my perspective cannot be expected to be my concern."[1] Rorty's understanding of the public, which is, in part, a result of a universalizing impulse for unity, is then both false in that it conceives of the public as being immune to, or unaccountable to, difference, and dangerous because it excludes a dialogue with difference.

Rorty's bracketing of the poststructuralist insistence on the acculturation of the self in his discussion of the self-as-artwork also makes his theory of the private unacceptable and insidious. In universalizing multiplicity he makes it seem as if the private is free from cultural and political constraints. But a poststructuralist understanding of our "private" images, concerns, needs, desires is no less a product of the dominant models of a particular society, culture, and history, than are our public ones. The difficulty is not keeping the "private" private, but in making it public (and the construction of the public is often also hidden from view). If the realm of the private is equated with the "merely aesthetic," with an "autonomous will," it is made impervious to political critique, resistant to change on a social level. Rorty's notion of the private must be resisted because it encourages, for example, the kind of thinking that refuses to see ideas of beauty, of desire, of normalcy, of intelligence, as being constituted within a public/political discourse and so subject to instrumental, or "normalizing" and "disciplinary" rationality. I mean, among other things, to be pointing out that these ideas relegated by Rorty to the private sphere are not just private poems—they affect and regulate the lives, both public and private, of the majority of the population (i.e., those whose interests are not served by the hegemony of bourgeois liberalism) in a *systematic* way. The fact that, in a very real sense, the images which circulate in a culture set the boundaries for our understanding of the possible kinds of lives we can lead, the fact that knowledge can, to borrow from Foucault, be seen as a function of power, makes it very difficult for us to formulate real choices about our private lives *unless* those images are brought out of the realm of the private and made public, are made part of a (though not necessarily the) dominant public discourse. And even then the choice of, or resistance to, the dominant knowledge regime is problematic.[2] The vocabulary out of which our private lives are built needs to be seen as having been constituted at a particular moment in history for particular purposes, and as having effects that go beyond one person's (or anyone in particular's) idiosyncratic vision. The insights of poststructuralism can be used to insist that aesthetic choices too are politically informed,[3] and my thesis is that such an understanding of the private (in Rorty's terms, "aesthetic") as political, and of the political insidiousness (and bias) of splitting the public and the private must be made a part of oppositional politics.

It is just such an insistence on the ubiquity of power, in my terms, of "politics," to which Foucault's thesis of power/knowledge speaks. Foucault has a properly poststructuralist understanding of our "private images," an understanding whose deconstruction of the public/private split provides a valuable tool for the formation of oppositional politics. Foucault is therefore to be valued as being more useful as a political thinker from the perspective of oppositional politics than either Lyotard, who shares his radical sympathies, or Rorty, who does not.

Lyotard's political goals are not unlike Foucault's. He would like his postmodernism to aid in the construction of oppositional politics. He argues against unreflective conformity and enforced performativity. His ideal political space would be one in which, to speak with the metaphor of another age, a thousand flowers bloom.

The problem with Lyotard, however, is that his universalization of terror forecloses on the possibility of achieving such a goal. He need not have offered a *theory* in the sense of a blueprint for "what ought to be done," but his writings do not even serve as useful tools for the program of oppositional politics. He tells us to adopt a model of agonistics, of paralogy, to resist consensus, to abjure community. Such exhortations tear down but offer no means for positive political construction. He argues that a well-working political system would be one which was structured around the goal of presenting the unpresentable. Yet this argument entangles him either in incoherence, for as he understands it, the unpresentable cannot be presented in a language we could understand, for if we understood it—it would have been terrorized by the present performative norms of rationality, or in mysticism, since the unpresentable exists as an Idea which can be intuited but never understood, or it entangles him in elitism, for the unpresentable can be understood only by the artist-intellectuals who are the only ones capable of escaping the clutches of modern (as opposed to postmodern) discourse.[4] The proponent of oppositional politics may sense that there is a kind of sympathy existing between her or his goals and the goals of Lyotard, but aside from confirmation of the feeling of frustration which arises from feeling that the dominant values, ideals, and images available within the culture are not one's own, she or he will get no help in articulating this frustration. In fact, in denying the political need for consensus and community, and arguing for agonistic and paralogical confrontations as properly constitutive of the norms of social exchange, and in equating all forms of power with terror, thereby making it impossible to present the unpresentable, the unintended consequence of Lyotard's theory is that it keeps this frustration at the level of the inarticulate. He does not allow us to know ourselves better, nor does his theory free a space for oppositional resistance.

Rorty fares no better, and in fact, as a model for oppositional politics, his theory is dangerous in a way that Lyotard's is not. Lyotard is not able to give us a methodology for demarginalization, for the articulation of resistant voices—at best he makes the voicing of marginalized others mystical or equivalent to a private language, at worst he retrenches into Kantianism and/or elitism—but Rorty's public/private split is more insidious: it self-consciously *institutionalizes* the marginalization, and so oppression, of discordant voices. Any suggestion for a reordering of society, for a critical reexamination of culture, or self-images or ideals, entails a theory of one sort or another, and all theories are relegated to the private and so are given the status of a "merely private poem." Oppositional voices are thus institutionally depoliticized and rendered impotent, by the public/private split.

Foucault's thesis of power/knowledge, his genealogizing of "norms" and his politicizing of everyday life, is meant to offer what Lyotard cannot and Rorty will not, viz., a tool for the use of oppositional resistance. His thesis of power/knowledge goes a long way toward providing an analysis helpful to oppositional struggles. And so, from the perspective of those who are marginalized, he is far in advance of Rorty. However, it is arguable that in itself, Foucault's thesis is no less mystifying than Lyotard's. His understanding of the self as an effect of disciplinary and normalizing power regimes forces one to be skeptical about the viability of a Foucauldian politics. Poststructural and postmodern politics has yet to be seen to offer a *constructive* political model.

The thesis of power/knowledge will be the focal point of the present chapter. I will argue that Foucault's thesis entails a recognition of the ubiquity of power and that this is a thesis that encourages imaginative reconstructions of everyday life along lines that are in keeping with the poststructural insight that subjectivity and intentionality are not prior to, but functions of forms of life and systems of language, and that they therefore do not constitute the world but are themselves elements of a linguistically disclosed reality. It is also in keeping with the poststructural demand for allowing the other to speak, and with the postmodern repudiation of all legitimizing discourse.[5] On the negative side, however, I will argue that Foucault's thesis of power/knowledge leaves no room for subjects of oppositional resistance. This is a problem which comes about with the tendency to equate power with terror, a tendency found totalized in Lyotard and present also in Foucault, though not perhaps consistently. (This is a point to which I will be returning later in this chapter.) I will be asking, then, whether Foucault's work can offer a viable oppositional *politics*. Along with this we will need to know whether Foucault is able to constitute resistance within the context of a political theory that thematizes the ubiquity of power; is he able to offer not merely a negative, but also a positive critique? In part, an affirmative answer to these questions depends on whether his theory offers or suggests a model of consensus and community which both resist the totalizing impulse which characterizes Rorty's defense of bourgeois liberalism, and is also resistant to the universalization of difference and terror, which is the bad side of Lyotard's resistance to traditional political theory and all legitimizing discourse.

Sketching Foucault

I will begin by offering an overview of Foucault's genealogical method and its consequent bearing on his understanding of power and knowledge. Such an overview will serve as a background and grounding for my discussion of Foucault's politics and for arguing his advance over Rorty.

Foucault came to view his early "archaeological" task of analyzing the internal logic of autonomous discourses as being inadequate because it did not place enough emphasis on the social practices and institutions in which such discussions were embedded. In works such as *Discipline and Punish* and *The History of Sexuality*, archaeology is replaced by "genealogy." The aim of genealogy is to uncover through the historical analysis of discontinuities (the moments at which social practices change) the ways in which individuals are constituted as subjects and objects of knowledge: "The history of the 'objectification' of those elements that the historians consider as objectively given . . . that is the sort of circle I want to try and investigate."[6]

Genealogical analysis seeks to disrupt the unity of familiar "natural" objects of our experience. Foucault sees his job as genealogist and intellectual, as one of providing a reexamination of evidence and assumptions. His goal is to "shake up habitual ways of working and thinking, to dissipate conventional familiarities, to re-evaluate rules and institutions and starting from this re-problematization, to participate in the formation of a political will."[7] The formation of such a political will is not carried out through theory and theoreticians, but by acting and actors. It is, Foucault says, "a matter of showing how social mechanisms up to the present have been able to work, how forms of repressions, constraint have acted, and then, starting from there, it seems to me, one [leaves] to the people themselves, knowing all the above, the possibility of self determination and the choice of their own existence."[8] Genealogy helps effect such a choice because its analysis problematizes truth; it problematizes the givens of our everyday existence by showing how those familiar, apparently actual or given objects of our experience—the self and our bodies (sexuality) as well as our social institutions (prisons, schools, hospitals, families) and scientific norms (sanity and insanity, health and illness) are objects produced in historically variable relations of power: "To grasp these effects [of power] as historical events—with what this implies for the question of truth [of the relationship between power and knowledge]— this is more or less my theme."[9]

One of the terms Foucault uses to describe the problematic of history and the construction of the present is "eventalization." By this he means,

> First of all, a breach of self-evidence. It means making visible a *singularity* at places where there is a temptation to invoke a historical constant, an immediate anthropological trait, or an obviousness that imposes itself uniformly on all. To show that things "weren't as necessary as all that"; it wasn't a matter of course that mad people came to be regarded as mentally ill; it wasn't self-evident

that the only thing to be done with a criminal was to lock him up, it wasn't self-evident that the causes of illness were to be sought through the individual examination of bodies; and so on. A breach of self-evidence, of those evidences on which our knowledges, acquiescences, and practices rest. This is the first theoretico-political function of "eventalization."

Secondly, eventalization means rediscovering the connection, encounters, supports, blockages, plays of forces, strategies, and so on that at a given moment establish what subsequently counts as being self-evident, universal and necessary. In this sense one is . . . effecting a sort of multiplicity or pluralization of causes.[10]

Genealogical analysis, or eventalization, thus treats the constitution of objects about which true or false statements can be made, "objects" such as the body, for example, as historical events. In so doing, genealogy replaces what has been seen to be unitary, necessary, and invariant with the multiple, contingent, and arbitrary. Its "theoretico-political" goal then is to contribute to changing people's ways of perceiving and doing things, to "participate in this difficult displacement of forms of sensibility and thresholds of tolerance." As Baynes and Bohman correctly point out, Foucauldian analysis makes us "critical of the presumed rationality of our discourses and practices"; it takes us behind the facade of universality and objectivity to reveal the operations of modern techniques of domination of which the modern self-examining, self-policing, self-disciplining—in short, "normal"—individual is a product.[11]

From the perspective of oppositional politics and the concern to resist normalization of dominant discourses, the most interesting, and useful, aspect of the genealogical method is its consequent understanding of power; genealogy reveals the extent to which we are the effects of power, for the "truth" that makes the laws, that produces the discourses which "decide, transmits and itself extends upon the effects of power" is itself a product of relations of power. So much so, that in the end "we are judged, condemned, classified, determined in our undertakings, destined to a certain mode of living and desiring," as a function of discourses of truth which are "bearers of specific effects of power."[12] This kind of determinism would seem to preclude any sort of freedom, any possibility for resistance, but this is not Foucault's conclusion. There is something, and he is not always clear on exactly what this something could be, given that he seems in passages such as these to be universalizing the effects of power, about the mechanisms of power which themselves produce the possibility, perhaps even the inevitability, of resistance.[13]

What resistance can mean, given his view of power, is an important question to which I will be returning, but for now, I am more concerned to note the fact that genealogy is meant to serve as a tool for that resistance (and this theme too will be returned to). A genealogical understanding of ourselves, our social institutions, and our practices reveals how the mechanisms of power come to be effectively incorporated into the social whole. Such an analysis is meant to suggest how the individual can also produce new effects of power.[14]

But what exactly is meant by "power"? Modern power in Foucault's formulation differs from all other forms of power in that it is "disciplinary" and "confessional"; its goal is normalization and the production of docile and useful bodies. In *Discipline and Punish* Foucault focuses on prisoners to show how discipline becomes self-regulating and in this sense is "inscribed" on the body. Instead of enforcing the repression of desires, carceral society produces bodies that signify the prohibitive law as the essence of their selves. The law never appears as external to the bodies it subjects and subjectifies. The very body then becomes both a product and agent of political power.

Foucault's point in *Discipline and Punish* and elsewhere is that modern power is so insidious because its power relations no longer operate openly as coming from a sovereign and demanding obedience. Instead, disciplinary and confessional forms of power mask themselves as forms of truth and knowledge—as, for example, sanity or insanity, as delinquency or sexuality. The particular form modern power takes is centerless—it is not, for example, located in the State or in any "unique source of sovereignty from which secondary and dependent forms would emanate"[15]—rather, it is for Foucault a "moving substrate of force relations which, by virtue of their inequality, constantly engender states of power, but the latter are always local and unstable. . . . Power is everywhere, not because it embraces everything, but because it comes from everywhere."[16] Power is "omnipotent,"[17] "ubiquitous:" it is "always already there."[18] The agents of this distinctively modern form of normalizing/disciplinary power include social scientists, social workers, psychiatrists, doctors, teachers, and the ordinary citizen who internalizes the categories and values of the power regime. It is these kinds of configurations of power/knowledge that are the target of Foucault's analysis in works such as *Discipline and Punish* or *The History of Sexuality*.

Genealogy, then, reveals not only the omnipresence of power, it also reveals its "productive" nature; power is not merely repressive, it doesn't just say no. It is also productive: "it induces pleasure, forms of knowledge, produces discourse. It needs to be considered as a productive network which runs through the whole social body, much more than a negative insistence which function is repressive."[19] This means that power is not the possession of subjects any more than knowledge is, for "power produces effects on the level of desire and also at the level of knowledge. Far from preventing knowledge, power produces it."[20] Power is thus seen as a "network" of relations which are responsible for the constitution of subjects as both products and agents of power: ". . . The individual is not a pregiven entity which is seized on by the exercise of power. The individual, with his identity and characteristics, is the product of a relation of power exercised over bodies, multiplicities, movements, desires, forces,"[21] and is therefore, not "the *vis-à-vis* of power," but "one of its prime effects."[22]

Thus, power does not extend from the top down, but instead operates from the bottom up.[23] This means that power is "capillary"—it circulates through the cells and extremities of the entire social body and operates on every level of social practice, social relations, and social institutions. I shall refer to this capillary view of power as "ubiquitous."[24] The political import of the thesis of the ubiquity of power becomes clear when contrasted with Rorty's exclusion of the private from the public. It is what makes Foucault attractive to, and useful for, oppositional politics, and it is the absence of such a thesis in Rorty which makes his work correspondingly useless and unattractive.

The debate between Rorty and Foucault: enlightenment vs. oppositional struggle

> . . . in contrast with the various projects which aim to inscribe Knowledges in the hierarchical order of power associated with science, a genealogy should be seen as a kind of attempt to emancipate historical knowledges from that subjection, to render them capable of opposition and of struggle against the coercion of a theoretical, unitary, formal and scientific discourse.[25] (Foucault, *Power/Knowledge*)

The most trenchant differences between Rorty and Foucault are outlined in this section. I suggest in this and the following section that the insidiousness of Rorty's implicit political program is highlighted against the background of Foucauldian critique.

Rorty wishes to maintain the status quo beneficial to North Atlantic democracies, and does so by banishing from public consideration or political seriousness any theory or voice which would threaten his preferred order since nothing can count against the progress it supplies us with. He argues that the drawbacks of liberal bourgeois society, including those ways in which it does not allow for self-creation, are overridden by the fact that "the selves shaped by modern liberal societies are better than the selves earlier societies created."[26] While it may be true that those patterns of acculturation liberal societies have imposed on their members take forms of which premodern societies had never even dreamed, Rorty is willing to see these constraints as being "compensated for by a decrease in pain."[27] As far as Rorty is concerned, then, J.S. Mill's suggestion that governments devote themselves to optimizing the balance between leaving people's private lives alone and preventing suffering, is "pretty much the last word."[28]

Foucault's genealogical deconstruction of the public/private is, on Rorty's view, both uncalled for and unnecessary. It is uncalled for since it encourages intrusion on other people's private poems and it is unnecessary, since the public humanist values of liberal societies allow for the greatest freedom of private expressions coincident with the greatest good for the greatest number.

Foucault, on the other hand, wishes to bring the private into the sphere of the public, effectively banishing the distinction. This would bombard the status quo with a multiplicity of oppositional voices; the "status quo" would be dethroned. Instead of a central regulating power structure producing regimes of truth, there would be many temporary and competing local power struggles. This brings to light the political nature of truth: for Rorty truth is synonymous with whatever works best to maintain the values of bourgeois liberalism, for Foucault, it serves to bring to light the "reality of possible struggles."[29] As Foucault says, "I would like to produce some effect of truth which might be used for a possible battle, to be waged by those who wish to wage it, in forms not yet to be formed and in organizations yet to be defined."[30]

For both then, following in the footsteps of Nietzsche, truth is created. For both "truth" aids a political ideal. The difference though is that while Rorty uses truth to silence difference, Foucault wields truth to promote it; the multiplicity of truths is emphasized, a multiplicity which he sees as existing in the public, and not just the private, sphere.

Foucault's commitment to multiplicity, and his distinction from Rorty on this point, is also evident in their respective conceptions of how the present ought to relate to the future. Foucault speaks to a yet-to-be-imagined future, but refuses to speak for it, since the forms of the future are as various as the multiple points of possible kinds of struggle. Rorty speaks for a segment of the present whose partiality he either discounts or ignores altogether. He does not speak to a future substantially different from the present, but imagines, to use Hegelian metaphors, the march of Spirit to have reached its final stage, or as Rorty himself puts it,

> I think that contemporary liberal society already contains the institu-
> tions for its own improvement—an improvement which mitigates
> the dangers Foucault sees. Indeed, my hunch is that Western social
> and political thought may have had the last *conceptual* revolution
> it needs.[31]

All that is left is to "expand the range of our present 'we.' "[32]

Foucault, on the other hand, views such an extension of the present as illegitimate and, I suppose one could even say, unjust: "to imagine another system is to extend our participation in the present system,"[33] and what is wrong with this can be stated in Lyotardian terms: it is terroristic, instead of allowing for serious difference, it forces confor- mity (normalization).

All of these differences between Rorty and Foucault can be boiled down to a different conception of the "we" they address, the "we" each aims to protect.

We liberals vs. we deviants

> I disagree with Foucault about whether in fact it is neces-
> sary to form a new "we." My principle disagreement with
> him is precisely over whether "we liberals" is or is not
> good enough.[34] (Rorty, *Contingency, Irony, Solidarity*.)

Let us reconsider Rorty's claim that Western, social, and political thought may have had the last conceptual revolution it needs, along with his statement that this is not to say that the world has had the last *political* revolution it needs.[35] Rorty is assuming here that what is at stake is always the diminution of cruelty and what is more controversial, that "cruelty" and its remedies are obvious and univocal. It is with this in mind that he claims that the unmasking which Foucault is so good at is "irrelevant."[36] But is it? Is it always the case that "power swaggers naked, and nobody is under any illusions"?[37]

Rorty is able to hold such a view because he does not see that power operates at the lowest extremities of the social body in everyday practice. Once power is seen, with Foucault, as being thus anchored in the multiplicity of "micropractices," in the social practices which comprise everyday life in modern society, divisions between the public and the private appear obsolete.

As a proponent of liberal humanists' values, Rorty champions the public/private distinction for its ability to protect autonomy and selfhood—as if subjectivity, autonomy, selfhood, creativity, pursuits of the good life, could be developed in isolation from the encroachment of the "public," of the political, of state and/or economic interests. But if modern power is as Foucault argues, if it is normalizing and disciplinary, then the notions to which the humanist appeals are integral components of the disciplinary regime; they are the very norms and objects through which discipline and normalization operate.

This is why Foucault mounts an attack against humanism. He sees humanism as comprising the totality of discourse through which Western citizens are denied the exercise of power and taught to submit to the power regimes already in place:

> Humanism invented a whole series of subjugated sovereignties: the soul (ruling the body, but subjected to God), consciousness (sovereign in a context of judgment, but subjugated to the necessities of truth), the individual (a titular control of personal rights subjected to the laws of nature and society), basic freedom (sovereignty within but accepting the demands of an outside world and "allied with destiny"). In short, humanism is everything in Western civilization that restricts *the desire for power*: it prohibits the desire for power and excluded the possibility of power being seized.[38]

The revolt against humanism is a revolt against all forms of subjugation. Such revolts cannot just be waged in the arena of class struggle, for power operates in spheres other than the economic—in social and cultural spheres as well. So political struggles do not simply entail a redress of economic forces, they must also be mounted against the hegemony of "culture." This is the form Foucault's own political struggle takes. The analysis of normalization in, for example, the *History of Sexuality, Volume I* is meant to aid in the breaking up of all the prohibitions that form and guide the development of a normal, rational, conscientious, and well-adjusted individual.[39] Relationships of power must be attacked "through the notions and institutions that function as their instruments, armature, and armor."[40]

Humiliation, which, as the reader will recall, is singled out by Rorty as constituting the worst form of cruelty one human being can inflict upon another, is a good example of the cultural process of normalization and discipline. Fear of humiliation teaches one to talk, act, dress, and think in ways consistent with the norms of bourgeois society, with the ideal already in place. It is thus no accident that Rorty picks on humiliation as being the worst form of cruelty; such a form of cruelty, along with the concomitant values it presupposes, are already inscribed within the domain of the liberal political doctrine. Being taught to fear humiliation is one of the ways the present society engenders discipline and forms and guides the development of a normal individual. There are different forms of cruelty whose eradication would have far more radical implications for present liberal capitalist societies—for example, what if the silencing of deviant voices were viewed as the worst form of cruelty? What if we refused the possibility of humiliation? (If I don't care about "fitting in," then having it pointed out that I don't will not be a cause of pain.)

The most important contribution of Foucault to oppositional discourse is that he would render meaningless the distinction between the public and the private: both the public and the private are the effects of power. The very production and reproduction of life itself in modern society is an effect of power, not the least of which is "biopower": population, health, urban life, sexuality . . . these too are objects of power/knowledge; these too are resources which are administered, cultivated, and controlled.[41] And if power is instantiated in mundane social practices and relations, then efforts to dismantle or transform the regime cannot ignore those practices and relations. The insightful consequences of Foucault's theory is this: since politics addresses itself to the control and maintenance of power regimes, *all social practices are potentially political*. This last is an insight which is not simply missing from Rorty's theory, his insistence on the public/private split prevents it from even being considered.

The realm of the political should not be predetermined; and in Foucault it is not. He frees us to ask of politics a whole series of questions not traditionally part of its statutory domain: questions about women, about relations between the sexes and forms of desire about medicine, about mental illness, about the environment, about minorities, about delinquency.[42] These kinds of questions are kept silent by the public/private distinction, but the ability to ask these sorts of questions, to see these issues as relevant to political and public concerns, is precisely what is at stake in a politics of difference. It is also what is at stake in Foucauldian politics. The liberation of the act of questioning plays a positive role: it poses a plurality of questions to politics rather than simply reinscribing the act of questioning in the framework of a preexisting political doctrine. Foucault's analysis of power and knowledge thus makes it possible for the silenced majority to begin to speak, to begin to formulate points of resistance.

Rorty's oversimplistic understanding of the sphere of political struggle acts to ensure the opposite. It keeps the status quo safe from genuinely critical questioning; it silences voices of genuine opposition for it does not allow the seriousness of attacks aimed at the heart of the normalizing and disciplinary regimes. His analysis of revolution does not go beyond localizing the source of power in the state or in the economy. He therefore sees Foucault's deconstruction of modern forms of power and the necessity of attacking such decentralized powers from the bottom up as being superfluous and "irrelevant."[43]

Foucault's capillary understanding of power refuses the adequacy of a thesis which centralizes power in the state or the economy. Seizure and transformation of state and/or economic power is not sufficient to dismantle or transform the modern power regime. Political struggles are not merely over who gets control of state or economic power, they are more accurately depicted as struggles over the actual ways in which power operates.

Viewing power as capillary, then, restructures our understanding of the purpose of revolutionary action. The goal is not the emancipation of truth from every system of power, "for truth is always already power," but of detaching truth from the forms of hegemony—economic, but also social and cultural—within which it operates at any given time.[44]

I have said that Foucault argues that power is anchored in the multiplicity of "micro-practices," the social practices which comprise everyday life in modern society, and it is just this that is necessary for oppositional politics. Contrary to Rorty's affirmation of the end of conceptual revolutions, Foucault's politicizing of everyday life and its implications for the multiplicity and plurivocality of power struggles, and that of concomitant formations of plural truths, keeps conceptual revolutions, and therefore opposition, an open possibility. Because Rorty's faith in a univocal, liberal bourgeois society leads him to believe that the need for conceptual revolution has ended, his idea of political struggle is one where what is being fought over is a way of better adjusting the same thought to the reality of things. But this goal of transformation does not go far enough, it does not yet see that "the reality of things" is an effect of disciplinary power:

> A transformation which would only be a certain manner of better adjusting the same thought to the reality of things, would only be a superficial transformation. On the other hand, from the moment one begins to be unable, any longer, to think things as one usually thinks them, transformation becomes simultaneously very urgent, very difficult, and altogether possible. . . .[45]

The difference between Rorty's ideal of politics which maintains the status quo, and Foucault's, which makes suspect the very existence of all normalizing structures, can be cashed out in terms of the "we" each is addressing. Rorty's "we" is the bourgeois liberal and the values he promotes are those which benefit that group. But the bourgeois liberal and the social order consonant with the protection of bourgeois values does not speak to the concerns of those marginalized by that social structure; for example, it benefits white propertied males at the expense of women, people of color, the middle and lower classes, the dispossessed.

Foucault's focus, on the other hand, is on all of those who are marginalized by liberal society, on all those who are the subjects of disciplinary power. His concern is to have his analysis of power/knowledge used as a tool for the voicing of resistance. Foucault can thus be characterized as a champion of deviancy—which is not to say that he need align himself with any particular deviant position—it is the *possibility* of deviant power struggles that is the point: the rebel is not necessarily innocent, the rebel's position not necessarily curative. One revolutionary group's success will not end the need for future revolution, will not end the need for conceptual revolution:

> One does not have to be in solidarity with [revolutionaries]. One does not have to maintain that these confused voices sound better than the others and express the ultimate truth. For there to be a sense in listening to them and in searching for what to say, *it is*

sufficient that they exist and that they have against them so much which is set up to silence them [emphasis mine].[46]

The point is that the "we" he speaks to are groups yet to be formed. They have yet to be formed because they have yet to break their silence.

Rorty criticizes Foucault for failing to appeal to any "we."[47] He argues that the "rhetoric of emancipation is absent from Foucault's work. Foucault's work "lacks an identification with any social context, any communication"; he "forbids himself the tone of the liberal sort of thinker who says to his fellow citizens: '*we* know that there must be a better way to do things than this; let us look for it together.' " There is, he concludes, "no 'we' to be found in Foucault's writings, nor in those of many of his French contemporaries."[48]

The question is not, however, whether Foucault fails to identify himself with any particular community, but whether there is anything inherent in his work—as I argued there was in Lyotard—to preclude the possibility of a "we": of consensus or community. For the worry behind Rorty's criticism is valid: without some form of community there cannot be an effective politics.

But it is one thing to allow for the formation of communities, and another to specify the form these communities must take. Whether or not Foucault's analysis *precludes* the formation of community will remain, for the moment, an open question. But it is true that he does not attempt to specify the form future communities must take, and this motivates much of the criticism against him. In part, this boils down to a contest between champions of the tradition and its dominated opponents.

I want, however, to come to Foucault's defense. His analysis of power paves the way for the multiplicity of yet-to-be-specified "we's" necessary for poststructuralist and oppositional politics.

Foucault and his critics

Foucault may not participate, as does Rorty, in the defense of any particular community, but this is intentional.[49] As Foucault sees it, the "true" discourses of Western culture have been constituted by the social and human sciences. These interested discourses have provided reasons, principles, and justification for those practices through which people have been classified, examined, trained, and formed as subjects. Both "conservative" and "progressive" prescriptions and programmings of behavior have been predicated on the assumed scientificity of such behaviors.[50]

Barry Smart is correct to note that "one of the principal objectives of Foucault's analysis is to contest the scientific hierarchizations of knowledges and the effects intrinsic to their power" implied in the scientific discourse of Western culture. Smart argues that Foucault's goal is not "the construction of a higher, more general and powerful theory." Rather he wishes to develop critiques of objectifying and subjectifying forms of power/knowledge in order to "reveal and thereby help reactivate the various forms of subjugated knowledges and local criticisms of 'an autonomous, non-centralized kind . . . whose validity is not dependent on the approval of the established regimes of thought.' "[51] That Foucault is not concerned with the approval of the established regimes of thought marks him as a *bête noire* of mainstream or liberal political theorists, and it in part explains why his politics offends critics such as Fraser, Habermas, Walzer, Taylor, and Rorty.[52] In their own way, each claims that since Foucault does not speak to a recognizable (or acceptable) "we," he cannot be a concerned or even effective critic, for he offers no program for "what ought to be done."

But Foucault's response is that this is a worry only for those operating within a certain set of traditional expectations. Foucault's epistemology is particularly attractive for those participating, or to those who would participate, in oppositional struggles. The epistemological attractiveness of Foucault's decentering of knowledges lies precisely in the fact that it bears little resemblance to current conceptions of knowledge and rationality, which, as Foucault enables us to appreciate, are intimately bound up with modes of domination. Whether or not his analyses are "effective" depends on the viewpoint of the "we" in question. It is true that he does not speak to those satisfied with the established order. From this perspective, he may in fact fail as a critic of reform. But suppose the "we" Foucault speaks to is not those happily operating within the boundaries of established norms; suppose he addresses the deviant . . . from that perspective his critique might in fact be suggestive of change, even if that change is outside of the establishment's idea of progress, and it is the deviant perpetrators of change he means to be addressing:

> It is true that certain people, such as those who work in the institutional setting of the prison—are not likely to find advice or instructions in my books that tell them "what is to be done." But my

project is precisely to bring it about that they "no longer know what to do," so that the acts, questions, discourses that up until then had seemed to go without saying became problematic, difficult, dangerous. This effect is intentional. And then I have some news for you: for me the problem of the prisoners isn't one for the social workers, but one for the prisoners. . . .[53]

It is no accident that those most critical of Foucault's political program are those happy operating within the framework provided by the mainstream, and those willing to find him useful are those who are looking for alternative voices. Whatever shakes up the carceral continuum is all right with Foucault—and this may well make defenders of the humanist tradition nervous.

Whether or not Foucault's work strikes one as "extraordinarily dry" as it strikes Rorty, is a function of one's perspective and one's commitments. Rorty thinks that Foucault's "dryness" is "produced by a lack of identification with any social context, and communication." But his dismissal of the seriousness of Foucault's work can be explained by the fact that it goes beyond Rorty's idea of the limits of acceptable political practice; it does not identify itself with a "project of reform"—it does not, in other words, accept the limits imposed by bourgeois liberalism.[54]

Michael Walzer argues that Foucault gives us no reason to believe the new codes and descriptions that will be produced will be any better than the ones we live with. But this misses the point. Again, the point is, it depends on the "we." Foucault refuses to identify with any particular "we." This is not his project, and in fact it is antithetical to his goal. But the "we's" he is sympathetic to and for whom his project is meant to be an aid are all those who would formulate resistances to the prevailing configurations of disciplinary power.

The critics I have mentioned want to fit Foucault into their idea of what counts as a useful theory. Nancy Fraser, for example, looks for a normative standpoint she can identify with, looks for Foucault's "justifications," for his "position."[55] Foucault is, from her point of view, successful, only if he can elaborate a "substantive, normative alternative to humanism." While she recognizes that "since his critique abjures traditional normative foundation and is therefore a critique rooted not in postmodern *theory*, but in postmodern *rhetoric*," she finds this unsatisfactory.

She also argues that in fact Foucault must be operating with humanist ideals; what else would explain his critique of normalization and carc-

erel society? Fraser argues that Foucault makes use of the very humanis-
tic rhetoric he claims to be rejecting. This is evident, she says, in his
"graphic description of the process of producing docile-useful bodies."
The fact that this is offensive" can only be explained by Foucault's
commitment to modern ideals of autonomy, dignity, reciprocity and
human rights."[56]

I do not wish to argue this point here. What I want to argue is that
even if she is right, it doesn't matter. Fraser, Rorty, et al., all criticize
Foucault because they take him to be doing something he is not. They
are trying to force him to conform to their notion of what a concerned
social critic must be—but he does not want to fit that mold.

Foucault would, I think, be willing to concede the point that his
way of thinking cannot fully escape the confines of his particular
culture—after all, he too is a product of modern power. Joseph Margolis makes an important point regarding this claim. Margolis's point
is that while Foucault is a poststructuralist, he is not a postmodernist.
As a poststructuralist, he is concerned with the "Other" victimized by
the efficiency of normalizing and disciplinary power. But the recovery
of the Other always takes place within a certain power structure, within
normalizing discourse. As Margolis so aptly notes: "the recovery of
the 'Other' *requires a parasitic use of language that is never merely
discursive though it will appear to be.*"[57] "Foucault," he goes on to
say, "introduces 'empiricist' and 'transcendental' discourse all right.
He *uses* it, aware that, in doing so, *he* is normalizing the distinctions
and claims he introduces. But he introduces it to subvert it. . . ."[58]
Margolis claims that Foucault's originality lies precisely in this recognition that "second-order legitimation [i.e., theory] of a discursive regime" is "itself subject to the effective 'power' that installs or produces
that very regime."[59] In other words, "we cannot abandon our own
order—even where we would attack it."[60] So even if, *pace* Fraser or
Habermas, it can be shown that Foucault does hold on to humanist
or legitimative ideals, this need not be seen as damaging to Foucault's
thesis. The important thing to consider is how he treats those ideals.
And what sets him apart from his critics is that he doesn't seek to
legitimate practices or discourses—he does not, as does Rorty, argue
that his values are universal or that they should shape or limit the
course of the future.

Insofar as he is a spokesman for bourgeois liberal society, and insofar
as he promotes the hegemony of that society by arguing that its success
has ended the need for conceptual revolutions, Rorty's humanist idea
of liberation is an ideal which operates against a transcendence of

domination. Labels such as "we liberals" and "we members of rich North American democracies" foster illusory unity that serves only to repress difference and social contexts. Rorty sees his role as one of expanding the range of "our" present we. Such a project is, he argues, an "end in itself."[61] But then Rorty's project and Foucault's project are diametrically opposed. And this is true not only for Rorty, but for all defenders of the liberal tradition.

The point I have been making in this section is that many of Foucault's critics do not take seriously his commitment to a politics of difference, to the project of creating the means by which marginalized voices can assert themselves—even if this means overthrowing the present power regime, along with the regime of truth and values. To understand Foucault is to appreciate his radical sympathies. It is to pay attention, and I come back to this again, to who the "we" is Foucault speaks to, and more particularly, why he refuses to speak *for* them.

On the question "What is to be done?"

> In my opinion you were the first—in your books and in the practical sphere—to teach something absolutely fundamental: the indignity of speaking for others. We ridiculed representation and said it was finished, but we failed to draw the consequences of this theoretical conversion—to appreciate the theoretical fact that only those directly concerned can speak in a practical way on their own behalf. (Deleuze in conversation with Foucault.)[62]

Foucault refuses to be a spokesman for any particular "we" because he is wary of his ability to transcend his particular normalizing discourse. We must take seriously his claim that to imagine another system is to extend our participation on the present system.[63] But if we take him seriously, then Rorty's and the others' criticism lose a great deal of their force: Foucault's point is that he cannot speak for others, nor does he wish to. He does not want to prescribe what ought to be done. He takes his embeddedness seriously:

> ... the intellectual discovered that the masses no longer need him to gain knowledge: they *know* perfectly well, without illusion; they know far better than he and they are certainly capable of expressing

themselves. But there exists a system of power which blocks, prohibits, and invalidates this discourse and this knowledge. A power not only found in the manifest authority of censorship, but one that profoundly and subtly penetrates an entire social network. Intellectuals are themselves agents of this system of power—the idea of their responsibility for "consciousness" and discourse forms part of the system. The intellectual's role is no longer to place himself "somewhat ahead and to the side" in order to express the stifled truth of the collectivity; rather it is to struggle against the forms of power that transform him into its object and instrument in the sphere of "knowledge," "truth," "consciousness," and "discourse."[64]

Foucault sees himself as being involved in "a struggle against power, a struggle aimed at revealing and undermining power when it is most invisible and insidious." The struggle is not to awaken consciousness, not to alert the masses to their "true" needs, "but to sap power, to take power; it is an activity conducted alongside those who struggle for power, and not their illumination from a safe distance."[65] Foucault, then, means his analysis of power to be used as a *tool* for those involved in struggles over power. The notion of theory as a toolkit means first that "the theory to be constructed is not a system, but an instrument, a *logic* of the specifics of power relations and the struggles around them," and secondly, "that this investigation can only be carried out step by step on the bases of reflection (which will necessarily be historical in some of its aspects) on given situations."[66] He agrees with Deleuze's assessment that one's books should be treated "as a pair of glasses directed to the outside; if they don't suit you, find another pair; I leave it to you to find your own instrument, which is necessarily an instrument for combat. A theory does not totalize; it is an instrument for multiplication. . . ."[67]

Foucault sees the problem of politics as setting differences into play[68] while respecting the multiplicity of "truth."[69] He therefore views his political role as an intellectual as one which seeks to provide oppositional voices with a tool for destabilization.[70] His analysis of power, then, is meant to be a tool for resistance. But offering his analysis of power as a tool for resistance does not mean he is offering a program of action or committing himself to any particular struggle: "I would like to produce some effects of truth which might be used for a possible battle, to be waged by those who wish to wage it, in forms not yet to be found and in organization yet to be defined."[71]

Foucault thus refuses to play the game his critics try to draw him into. He refuses to take a prophetic stance, to prescribe for others what action they should take:

> ... it seems to me that "what is to be done" ought not to be determined from above by reformers be they prophetic or legislative, but by a long work of comings and goings, of exchanges, reflections, trials, different analyses. ... And it is because of the need not to tie down ... or immobilize ... that there can be no question for me of trying to [say] "what is to be done."[72]

The most important thing, he claims, is not to bury those seeking an answer to the question "what is to be done" under the weight of prescriptive or prophetic discourse:

> The necessity of reform mustn't be allowed to become a form of blackmail serving to limit, reduce, or halt the exercise of criticism. Under no circumstances should one pay attention to those who tell you, "Don't criticize, since you're not capable of carrying out a reform." Critique doesn't have to be the premise of a deduction that concludes: This then is what needs to be done. It should be an instrument for those who fight, those who resist and refuse what is. Its use should be in the process of conflict and confrontation, essays in refusal. It doesn't have to lay down the law for the law. It isn't a stage in a programming. It is a challenge directed to what is.[73]

The problem is one for the subject who acts; the real will be transformed "when critique has been played out in the real, not when reformers have realized their ideas."[74]

Rorty serves as an example of the kind of theoretician Foucault is warning against.

Rorty demands of critique that it give "concrete alternatives and programs."[75] The problem with this can be argued from more than one angle. For one, what is counted as a serious or viable alternative or program is predetermined: it must be one which furthers the goal of expanding the values of bourgeois culture, of the present "we" into the future. This has the consequent effect of silencing any alternative not acceptable to the current idea of the normal or rational. And the form of critique is limited in yet another way: it is made the property of the ironist intellectual.[76] The non-intellectuals would not be raised to participate in the sorts of language games which would enable them to have doubts about the contingencies they happen to be. Rorty thus on the one hand demands that critique give concrete alternatives and programs, and on the other, denies the people the possibility of cultivating the kind of imagination needed for such critique. Liberal culture, he claims, neither could, nor ought, to be a culture whose public rhetoric was ironist: "I cannot imagine a culture which socializes its youth in such a way as to make them continually dubious about their own process of socialization."[77] And here the differences between Rorty and Foucault are both striking and obvious; Rorty disqualifies precisely those forms of knowledge which interest Foucault: namely deviant and destabilizing knowledges.

Foucault would argue that the alternatives and programs given by *critique* in Rorty's sense would simply amount to regurgitating acceptable and pre-formed effects of the knowledge and power that invests present scientific discourse. Expanding the present "we" into the future amounts to a program of normalization. The kind of knowledge he is encouraging is altogether different. It is,

> . . . the set of knowledges that have been disqualified as inadequate to their task or insufficiently elaborated: naive knowledges, located low down on the hierarchy, beneath the required level of cognition or scientificity. I also believe that it is through the reemergence of these low-ranking knowledges, these unqualified, even directly disqualified knowledges (such as that of the psychiatric patient, of the ill person . . . of the delinquent, etc.), and which involve what I would call a popular knowledge, but is on the contrary a particular, local, regional knowledge, a differential knowledge incapable of unanimity and which owes its force only to the harshness with which it is opposed by everything surrounding it—that is through the reappearance of this knowledge, of these local popular knowledges, these disqualified knowledges, that criticism performs its work.[78]

And even for himself, for the "ironist intellectuals" if you will (though I imagine Foucault would hate having that label attached to him, given its formulation in Rorty's corpus), he would spurn the claim that the validity of critique depends upon its ability to suggest "concrete alternatives," to specify what is to be done. Foucault genuinely struggles to participate in multiplicity—difficult as it may be to escape the totalizing effect of normalization. His work, he says, is an attempt to modify what he thinks, and even what he is; "to work is to undertake something other than what one has thought before."[79]

Foucault's goal, then, is not to provide a theory of what ought to be done. He has no wish to formulate a global, systematic theory, but only to analyze the specific mechanisms of power, to locate connections and extensions, to build little by little strategic knowledges. He feels that such analyses will aid revolutionary struggles because he believes that when struggles are provided with an adequate logic of their history and their effects, hegemony over the left cannot be successful. Foucault sees everything as being an effect and product of power.

This is analogous to the domination of phrase regimes talked about in Lyotard; because everything is formulated within the domain of a phrase and a phrase is both the "effect of power" and exclusionary of other powers, it is seen by Lyotard as a mark of terror. It is impossible then to locate within Lyotard the voice of resistance; it is as if his thesis of the terrorizing by "phrase regimes" forces him to conclude that to speak is already to be co-opted, and this is why the presentation of the unpresentable is totally mystified. Foucault, on the other hand, at least claims to be able to both postulate the omnipresence and ubiquity of power, even as inscribed on our very bodies, and still allow for the possibility of resistance and oppositional transformation. The question, though, is how? How can he both universalize the domination of subjectless power and still leave space for the empowerment of marginalized voices? In fact he sometimes uses his refusal to speak for oppositional voices as a shield to hide behind; we cannot allow his refusal to speak for marginalized voices to excuse him from addressing the difficult questions regarding resistance—made even more difficult, given the context of power in which resistances arise and are said to be products.

This leads us then to consider more closely his notion of resistance. Granted, he need not provide a blueprint for the form oppositional struggles must or should take, still, his thesis of the ubiquity of normalizing and disciplinary power, along with its implication for his theory of the subject as an effect and also the vehicle of such power, forces us to ask questions such as: How is resistance possible, where does it come from, why would it arise? How can we affect conscious choices for resistance or subvert those powers which both constitute and oppress it? Does Foucault's analysis of the ubiquity of power eliminate reference to a thinking/willing subject who might motivate resistances?

In short, the thesis that "we cannot abandon our own order, even where we would attack it," renders Foucault's theory of power problematic for the possibility of resistance, and an evaluator of Foucault interested in the formation of oppositional struggles, and the voicing of marginalized voices, can both respect his refusal to shape those struggles while at the same time refusing to thereby be put off from demanding a more constructive (or even coherent) notion of resistance and transformation from a power regime to which we are subjected, to one we control.

Resistance and the subjects of opposition

There exist in Foucault's theory of resistance many unresolved tensions, among which is the tension which exists between his thesis that resistance is an inevitable consequence of power, and his belief that self-conscious subjects are the necessary catalyst for resistance. This last assertion is further complicated by the fact that if subjects are merely the effect of power, then self-consciousness is at best problematic. For example, his thesis that the subject is merely the effect of power invites the following question: how can, or why would, subjects which are the effects of power also subvert it?

While Foucault does mean to leave open the possibility for seeing self-conscious subjects as necessary to resistance, he does not do much to explain how such self-consciousness is possible, or why resistance would result in the transformation of power—and it is not enough of an excuse to say that this is a function of his unwillingness to prescribe what ought to be done.

To begin from the relation of power to resistance. Foucault believes that for every form in which power is exercised and applied there exist corresponding forms of resistance. This holds, even though resistances are themselves always inscribed within relations of power:

> Where there is power, there is resistance, and yet, or rather consequently, this resistance is never in a position of exteriority in relation to power. Should it be said that one is always "inside" power, there is no "escaping" it, there is no absolute outside where it is concerned, because one is subject to the law in every case? . . . This would be to misunderstand the strictly relational character of power relationships. Their existence depends on a multiplicity of points of resistance: these play the role of adversary, target, support, or handle in power relations. These points of resistance are present everywhere in the power network . . . there is a plurality of resistances, by definition, they can only exist in the strategic field of power relations. But this does not mean that they are only a reaction or rebound, forming with respect to the basic domination an underside that is in the end always passive, doomed to perpetual defeat. Resistances do not derive from a few heteronomous principles; but neither are

they a lure or a promise that is of necessity betrayed. They are the odd term in relations of power; they are inscribed in the latter as an irreducible opposite. . . . And it is doubtless the strategic codification of these points of resistance that makes a revolution possible.[80]

This gives us a summary of Foucault's theory of resistance in its relation to power. But how much does this description really tell us? It seems to hold out hope for the possibility of meaningful resistance even though resistance itself is always inscribed within those very relations of power it opposes. But I want to ask, "How exactly is this possible?" And on the face of it, at least, Foucault does not do more than merely state the relation of resistance to power as one of logical entailment. This leaves Foucault open to the charge that his is a world "in which things move, rather than people, a world in which subjects become obliterated or, rather, recreated as passive subjects."[81] In fact, it seems as if power/resistance follows an inevitable kind of materialist logic: wherever there is power, there will also be resistance; this is simply the logic of the situation. This is rather like a political application of Newton's third law: For every action there is an equal and opposite reaction. But can this law be applied to people? What reason does Foucault give for believing it can? And even if resistance is logically entailed by power, what does this make of resistance? Can we get from resistance to purposive *transformation*?[82]

In fact, though in informal discussions and interviews Foucault speaks as a revolutionary, as a *theorist* Foucault gives us reason *not* to be optimistic about the possibility of resistance and transformation.

Foucault states in the passage quoted above, that the existence of power "depends on a multiplicity of points of resistance," that resistance "can only exist in the strategic field of power relations." But this means that resistance is co-opted for the purposes of disciplinary and normalizing regimes of power, and is evidence of the fact that resistance need not result in transformation.

And in fact, Foucault is not wrong. We see this co-opting of resistance all the time. Enough white middle-class women objected to being confined to the role of housewife for it to have become the norm for those women to find jobs outside of the home. But, far from changing the basic power structure, the phenomenon of women in the workplace has served to strengthen it. The male-dominated society hasn't given much up—women are still responsible for the household; government has not taken on the responsibility of making day care available to all, it has not sufficiently altered the workplace to accommodate demands for maternity (much less demands for paternity) leave, women are still not given equal pay for equal work, etc., it would not then be surprising if these women "chose" to go back to being housewives. The dominant power regime assures a no-win situation. If women work, more can be produced, and two-income families are able to spend more in an inflationary age than a single-income family would. On the other hand, if women are forced to go back to being housewives, the patriarchal power regime wins by having its values reinforced. Either way the dominant power regime is able both to benefit from, and deflect, resistance.[83] Or one could take the example of how resistances are used as a target to strengthen the hold of the dominant powers by unifying the people against a common enemy. This is seen in the war against drugs and in the homophobia grown up around the fear of AIDS. It was also dramatically illustrated a few winters back in the windows of Macy's department store in New York City, when they made the "homeless look" a fashion: mannequins were featured promoting shoes that were made to look like tattered rags. If homelessness can become a fashion, the horror evoked by seeing actual people in real rags will be defused. The protests of the homeless will then fall on deaf ears. And of course, the examples could easily be multiplied.

Resistance is also made problematic at the level of desire. Since we are formed by strategies of power we may well identify our interests with the interest of that very power which was formulated to oppress us. This is why Susan Bordo argues that a Foucauldian analysis of the strategic uses of power force us to question the integrity of our understanding of our oppositional realities. She is right to argue that Foucault "constantly reminds us that the results of individual interest and desire do not always lead where imagined and may often sustain unintended and unwanted configurations of power."[84] Foucault's analysis of power forces all marginalized voices to be alert to the possible co-opting of their particular consciousness. Bordo asks the question Foucauldian analysis makes worrisome: "Could feminist gender-skepticism, in all its multifaceted 'deployment' (to continue the Foucauldian motif), now be operating in the service of the reproduction of white male knowledge/power?"[85] We must be on the lookout to recognize the ways even defiant alternatives are co-opted.

Bordo's question is made even more urgent by Foucault's notion of resistance, of the seizure of power, because he takes the position that one can take power only by recognizing it—one can shape alternative power regimes only by seeing how we are the effect of present ones (this is the positive hope for genealogy). This is what he means by saying

> What I want to do . . . is to work out an interpretation, a reading of a certain reality, which might be such that on the one hand, this interpretation could produce some of the effects of truth; and on the other, these effects of truth could become implements within possible struggles. . . . Deciphering a layer of reality in such a way that the lines of force and the lines of fragility come forth; the points of resistance and the possible points of attack; the paths marked out and the shortcuts. It is the reality of possible struggles that I want to bring to light.[86]

But here certain problems begin to intrude. If disciplinary power feeds off of resistance, if it "annexes" the counter-discourses that have developed,[87] how can resistance be made genuinely subversive (how can it help being co-opted by the dominant power structures)? How can resistance be strategically codified—especially if the codes are always the products of normalization (or phrase regimes)?

At the very least, what such resistances require are subjects who are self-conscious about the effects of power. But this self-consciousness does not come easy.

Foucault often writes as if power constitutes the very individuals upon whom it operates:

> The individual is not to be conceived as a sort of elementary nucleus, a primitive atom, a multiple and inert material on which power comes to fasten or against which it happens to strike. . . . In fact, it is already one of the prime effects of power that certain bodies, certain gestures, certain discourses, certain desires, come to be identified and constituted as individuals.[88]

But if, as this thesis implies, individuals are *wholly* constituted by the power/knowledge regime Foucault describes, how can discipline be resisted in the first place? (Unless it comes about as an inevitable moment in the march of . . . but no, this is a very unfoucauldian thesis.) If individuals are wholly constituted by the power/knowledge regime, then it would make no sense to talk about resistance to discipline. As Sandra Lee Bartky notes, Foucault seems sometimes on the verge of depriving us of a vocabulary in which to conceptualize the nature and meaning of resistance.[89] And where he suggests the possibility of an alternative vocabulary, his thesis that individuals "with his identity and characteristics [are] the product of a relation of power exercised over bodies, multiplicities, movements, desires, forces"[90] must leave us skeptical about the possibility of alternative vocabularies.

If the subject is "constituted through practices of subjugation," then what sense can we make of the claim that it is also constituted "through practices of liberation, of freedom ... starting, of course, from a certain number of rules, styles, and conventions that are found in the culture"?[91] This grossly begs the question: how does one start from the rules, styles, and conventions of a disciplinary and normalizing culture and end up with practices of liberation and freedom?

Foucault never provides us with the missing steps, and in fact, has given us powerful reasons to suppose practices of "liberation" and "freedom"—even if these are liberations from one power regime to another—are impossible.

The difficulty of finding the possibility of a revolutionary vocabulary is not a problem peculiar to Foucault; it haunts many revolutionary proponents of poststructuralist politics. We have seen this in Lyotard's notion of the "unpresentable," which denotes his frustration over the cultural and scientific hegemony of language. This is also true of French feminists Luce Irigaray and Julia Kristeva, both of whom suggest that Western cultural traditions are univocally masculinist, and that the phallocentric discourses of these cultural traditions offer no place for women to speak out except insofar as they speak in ways predetermined by men.[92] Jana Sawicki argues the consequence of this viewpoint: "refusal of these subject positions leaves women with no alternatives but to speak in a masculine voice, or be silent."[93] Sawicki says that Foucault offers "a slightly more optimistic view of the relationship between language and power, for he rejected the view that the power of phallocentric discourse is total. Discourse is ambiguous and plurivocal, it is a site of conflict and contestation. Thus, women can adopt and adapt it to their own ends."[94] But this does not, I think, provide a good enough defense of Foucault. It is not obvious that discourse for Foucault *is* plurivocal. Certainly it isn't if one refers to *Discipline and Punish*, and though it might be argued that *The History of Sexuality* provides for the possibility of plurivocal discourse, this needs to be argued. At any rate, what we want to know is how it is possible for discourse to be multiple in the right way, i.e., in a way that allows for genuinely oppositional discourse and purposive transformation.

The thesis that phallocentric discourse is not total depends upon the existence of genuine loci of resistances. And even if we did not require that these points of resistance were not themselves instances of power, the question would still remain: how are the subjects of disciplinary and normalizing power regimes able to break out of the constraints of power? What tools do they have that are not already co-opted by (codified within) those very power regimes they are trying to resist?

Given that subjectivity is constituted through disciplinary practices and rationalizing discourses and is an effect of patriarchal, racist, and classist society, it could be said that Foucault cannot account for the fact that oppositional discourses do, in fact, appear. For while on the one hand, Foucault thinks that resistance requires subjects capable of acting in self-conscious and regulatory ways—the hoped-for practical application of his genealogical analyses of power presupposes the belief that because human practices are made they can be unmade, "of course, assuming we know how they were made"[95]—on the other hand, his thesis that resistance only exists in strategic fields of power relations where those relations of power are conceived of as disciplinary and normalizing, makes it unlikely that there can be regulatory or even self-conscious subjects of resistance. Furthermore, while his analysis may enable us to see ourselves as the objects of those relations of power which have made us what we are (and have made the world what it is), it does not help us to see how we can be the makers of new histories—how Foucault can begin with resistance and end up with self-conscious transformation.

Foucault's thesis is further muddied if we consider passages like the one quoted above in which he seems to be implying that the necessary and *sufficient* catalyst for resistance is self-conscious subjects. When speaking of his role, Foucault says that by uncovering the multiple effects of power he thereby aids the formation of multiple points of resistance—once we see not just that, but *how* forms of rationality and formations of the subject rest upon a foundation of human practices, once we know how these are made, he believes it then becomes possible for them to be unmade. This possibility rests upon subjects becoming aware of the multiple effects of power.

But it is not obvious that resistance *will* follow upon awareness of the effects of power. And the inference is even more unlikely if we take seriously the thesis that the subject and her or his identity is *entirely* a product of disciplinary and normalizing discourse.

If our personal identity is bound up with the interests of domination, radical critiques may in fact be seen as the threat to be resisted. Speaking to this point, Sandra Lee Bartky asks the following, I think, striking question: given that feminist critiques have pointed out the ways in which women's identities have been formed as a result of disciplinary and normalizing discourses, why isn't it the case that all women are feminists? She suggests, in keeping with Foucault's view of subjects as the effects of power, that the reason is that this identity is all we have; disciplinary power has formed our very idea of the feminine and has inscribed its power in the female body. All women, she says, have internalized patriarchal standards of bodily acceptability, which in turn have determined our sense of mastery and competence. She goes on to argue that women may very well be reluctant to part with the rewards of compliance, and that many women will resist the abandonment of an aesthetic that defines what they take to be beautiful. And then there is the fact that our culture has structured our options so that they will appear to be limited to the category of either the masculine or the feminine. To give up one's sense of oneself as female, then, might be felt as equivalent to giving up one's very self.[96] His theory of resistance notwithstanding, this is not an unfoucauldian conclusion.

So even if being alerted to the productive effects of power *could* result in attempts to oppose the hegemony of the dominant power regime, the resister who would refuse to be part of that regime is left with the difficult personal, psychological, epistemological, and also the difficult *political* question of who she might be. Foucault's analysis of power might lead the disadvantaged to want to formulate alternatives to the subjugating power regime, but it also implies the impossibility of this, since the question of being a woman—or any unco-opted, "deviant" identity—has been made more difficult by Foucault than we might have originally thought, for to refer to an identity is not just to refer to a social category, but to a felt sense of self. I find in Foucault no reason for revolting against oneself, and even more problematic from the standpoint of oppositional politics, no strategy for recovering an empowered, oppositional self.

The point can also be made on a larger scale: the political effectiveness of resistance for Foucault comes not from the standpoint of community, but from the standpoint of the subject, this despite passages coincident with the postmodernist demand for its deconstruction. But I would argue that the possibility of becoming conscious of subjugation, and the possibility of articulating marginalized voices and of formulating oppositional struggles, depend not on the self-consciousness of an autonomous subject, but on subjects-in-community, and so, on the *articulation* of community. There are times when similarity is more important than difference (this point will be developed more fully in the last chapter).

At his worst, Foucault's pluralism, which results from his insistence on the proliferation of localized power struggles—not only intersubjectively, but also interpersonally—keeps him from allowing for a subject sufficiently coherent to form communities of active resistance and transformation. We saw this in Lyotard's paralogistic and agonistic model of politics. We see this again in Foucault's commitment to the confrontational omnipresence of power and its concomitant destabilizing effect of the subject, evident in such passages as "there aren't any immediately given subjects of the struggle . . . who fights against whom? We all fight each other. And there is always within each of us something that fights something else."[97] Since the individual is nothing but the effects of power, it is better, he thinks, to speak of the subjects of struggle not as "individuals," but as "sub-individuals" always at war with their own values. But if the very self is thus fragmented into antagonistic sites of power, then he is no better able to admit consensus and community than was Lyotard.

It is this kind of conclusion that leads those engaged in oppositional struggles to repudiate the viability of postmodern politics. This is true, for example, of some feminists who consider Foucault, and postmodernism in general, to be disadvantageous for oppositional struggles:

> The postmodern project, if seriously adopted by feminists, would make any semblance of a feminist politics impossible—to the extent that feminist politics is bound up with a specific constituency or subject, namely women, the postmodernist prohibition against subject-centered inquiry and theory undermines the legitimacy of a broad-based organized movement dedicated to articulating and implementing the goals of such a constituency.[98]

Without a subject there can be no locus of resistance and without subjects coherent enough to form coalitions there can be no force to resistance.

And yet he doesn't always go this far. It is also clear that Foucault sees himself as participating in the formation of oppositional consciousness—in the formation of the consciousness of oppositional subjects—and that he sees such subjects as necessary for the project of the instantiation of new regimes of power formed from the standpoint of subjugated knowledges.

Unfortunately, where he allows for agents of struggle, these agents are "subjects" in an uncomfortably familiar sense of the word, and despite his advances over Rorty, this signifies yet another of those totalizing impulses which mask the viewpoint of the bourgeois male. There are (even if he doesn't say how—and this points to tensions which can be said to exist between Foucault's modern and postmodern tendencies) times in Foucault's writings where he posits the existence of subjects coherent enough to form coalitions, some of which coalitions will even, he says, be "permanent" [sic]. But, as he sees it, the first and last components of these coalitions will be "individuals,"[99] and this doesn't get us away from the bourgeois individualism which has dominated modern patriarchal, racist, and classist power regimes.[100] It also does not, therefore, adequately reflect how we come to achieve the self-consciousness necessary for oppositional political struggle.

On this point Lacanian theory proves instructive. It helps feminist theory articulate the ways in which the very notion of the subject is a masculine prerogative within the terms of culture. As Judith Butler notes,

> The paternal law which Lacanian psychoanalysis takes to be the ground of all kinship and all cultural relations not only sanctions male subjects, but institutes their very possibility through the denial of the feminine. Hence, far from being subjects, women are variously, the Other, a mysterious and irrecoverable lack, a sign of the forbidden and irrecoverable maternal body, or some unsavory mixture of the above.[101]

I would argue (though this is not the place for it) that Lacan's universalization of patriarchy goes too far. However, it does suggest that the traditional conception of the subject *is* necessarily patriarchal. The "traditional" subject I have in mind is the *autonomous* subject. *This* subject is a masculine cultural prerogative from which women, and also those with non-bourgeois values, have been excluded. This subject is "always already masculine" because it represses the importance of *dependency* in its very construction. The first step in recovering a female subject—and my intuition is that this would also be a first step in the recovery of any other oppositional subject which would abjure the values of possessive individualism—would be to acknowledge the necessity of the subject-in-dependency, or to use terms more consistent with my thesis, the necessity of subjects-in-community. Unfortunately, where he allows for a subject, Foucault's subject remains the subject of the bourgeois male.

Foucault's insights regarding the omnipresence of power should have led him to insist, in a way that he unfortunately did not, that since one's identity is always already the prime effect of power, it is always more than a personal question.[102] In failing to insist on this, Foucault makes an important mistake—and an important *political* mistake, for in the formation of resistance, of oppositional consciousness, I would argue that it is necessary to seek others out: to reconstruct, revitalize one's identity in community with others.

Foucault misses this point because he does not do enough to differentiate between effects of power. Laurie Hicks is correct to stress that "the effects of power vary depending upon one's place in the [power] network."[103] I would take this one step further and suggest that the very same strategy can be seen as both repressive and liberating. This can be seen in various strategic theories of the subject. For example, while it is true that the theory of the subject can be seen as one more instance of the repressive effects of patriarchal power, there are times at which it is strategically important to insist on the availability to oppositional theory of a coherent and unified subject. Oppositional struggles have both a critical and a constructive component. The ways in which their voices have been marginalized must be uncovered in order that alternative identities can be built. On the side of critique, feminist criticism can appeal to the destabilization of the subject as a useful tactic in the exposure of masculine power, and, as noted by Butler, ". . . in some French feminist contexts, the death of the subject spells the release or emancipation of the suppressed feminine sphere, the specific libidinal economy of women, the condition of *écriture féminine.*"[104]

However, the constructive task of oppositional politics is to remake the future in terms of new subjectivities—to "construct the subjectivity of the Other." If this is the case, then the deconstruction of the subject can also be seen as a threat. All marginalized voices fighting for empowerment should be sympathetic to Nancy Hartsock's concern:

> Somehow it seems highly suspicious that it is at the precise moment when so many groups have been engaged in "nationalisms" which involve redefinitions of the marginalized Others that suspicions emerge about the nature of the "subject," about the possibilities for a general theory which can describe the world, about historical

"progress." Why is it that just at the moment when so many of us who have been silenced begin to demand the right to name ourselves, to act as subjects rather than objects of history, that just then the concept of subjecthood becomes problematic?[105]

When Lyotard and Foucault deny the possibility of coherent subjects, when they repudiate consensus and community, it can be argued that their postmodern theories merely reproduce the effects of Enlightenment theories; the result of theories which deconstruct subjects is to deny the marginalized to participate in defining their interests, goals, desires—to construct a new voice.

Foucault emphasizes, and sometimes totalizes, the repressive effects of power (critique or theory) at the expense of its potential for liberation (construction), and this deemphasis on liberatory practices makes him suspect from the perspective of the disempowered.

In *The History of Sexuality* Foucault characterizes confessional practices which aim at self-disclosure and self-discovery as aiding the interests of domination and social control. Indeed, as Jana Sawicki notes, "Foucault was suspicious of most efforts to tell the truth about oneself." But this is only one side of the equation.

If one's alternative identity is yet to be established, yet to be codified into strategic discourses, then one needs to talk about oneself, to share and compare personal experiences.[106] Since the subject is an effect of multiple community formation, alternative subjects can only be formulated within the discourses of alternative communities. This is to claim that there are no individuals, in the traditional sense and that the traditional autonomous subject must be replaced by the concept of subjects-in-community.

Jana Sawicki aptly summarizes the tactical use of confessional practices:

> While self-refusal may be an appropriate practice for a privileged white male theorist like Foucault, it is less obviously strategic for feminist and other disempowered discourses. As women, most of us have been taught to efface ourselves as a matter of course. It has been suggested that anonymous was a woman. The absence of a sense of self, of one's values and authority, and of the legitimacy of one's needs and feelings is a hallmark of femininity against which feminism has struggled. One principal aim of feminism has been to build self-esteem—the sense of self-certainty and identity which are necessary for developing an oppositional movement. Telling our stories to one another has been an important part of this process.

> It could even be argued that feminist psychotherapies which cultivate self-preoccupation and self-assertion have benefitted the women's tendencies to lose themselves in others, particularly male others. Moreover, if we look at the role that feminist psychotherapy has played in uncovering the scandal of incest and physical abuse, then we may be forced to conclude that telling the truth about oneself can indeed disrupt patriarchal power relations. *This is particularly true if this truth is shared, analyzed and strategically deployed*[107] [emphasis added].

I would concur with Sawicki that "some forms of self-preoccupation are more politically suspect than others. The retreat into oneself can represent an escape from political reality, or it can help one get clear about the conditions governing one's choices and thereby free one up for new ways of thinking, new choices." But I would emphasize, in keeping with the themes of poststructuralism (and this is why I think there are tactical reasons to engage with poststructuralism) that self-preoccupation is also necessarily an identification with some form of community—there are no subjects in isolation—but that doesn't mean there are no subjects which are not the effects of the dominant power. Confessional practices can help one identify oneself as an unhappy product of domination, and so help one form new communities to identify with, even if these alignments are temporary and the self-identity they speak to is partial.

Foucault may be correct to point out that our bodies have been made docile and obedient, but this has political force only when we realize that domination is not personal and idiosyncratic, but represents the strategic domination of, and has been instrumental in, the identity formation of an identifiable group, such as women, for example. One may not see that one's eating disorder is the result of a pain and the attempt at the formation of an alternative "language" (a "language-body" to use Mark Anderson's description[108]) until the phenomena of anorexia and bulimia come to light as the result of shared discovery. What has always seemed "natural" can come to be seen as unnatural and thereby as possible to resist, in the process of telling one's story and comparing one's experiences with others. Sometimes what one has not noticed as a pain in oneself or as an alternative to the confines of dominant discourses is seen clearly as a pain and also as a new "language" when reflected in the experience of others.[109] And though there are many ways in which each individual is dissimilar from the next and is oneself not a site of a single narrative, noticing the points at which we *are* similar has strategic political purposes.

Foucault reconsidered

In summary of this chapter, I conclude that on the positive side, Foucault's analysis of power allows us to see all social practices, the "private" as well as the "public" as potentially political. This leaves the realm of the political open to a myriad of reconsiderations, reshapings, and possibly resistances. Foucault frees us to ask of politics a whole series of questions not traditionally considered part of its domain, and since the "tradition" is the tradition of white propertied males, he frees us to consider politics from the perspective of the marginalized other. Foucault's program is coincident with the program of oppositional politics precisely because it is crucial to oppositional politics that the realm of the political not be predetermined—it must always remain open to debate and fundamental, even "conceptual" change.

Foucault's genealogy aids oppositional politics because he participates in liberating the act of questioning. Rorty's bias toward the ironist intellectual forecloses on such liberation. Lyotard would have liked to, but was unable to see how to open a space for such liberation; his theory remains insignificant for the purposes of oppositional struggles. Foucault's genealogy does succeed in offering a *tool* (even if not a *theory*) for the liberation of questioning, and so, it is an aid for the assertion of the Other.

Genealogy problematizes truth, politics, everyday familiar objects: personal "objects" such as the self and the body, "private objects" such as the family and education, public "objects" such as the sciences and the legal institution. Within the Foucauldian framework, these are all seen as objects produced within historically variable relations of power—they are all, in other words, subject to being understood politically.

Foucauldian analysis does, then, create a breach in self-evidence: it brings to light the fact that things we might never have considered as being objects of power—things such as the body (and its "docility" and "usefulness") or sexuality—are objects that have been made. This does offer us the suggestion that they can also be unmade. One can take power only by recognizing it.

If power is instantiated in mundane social practices and relations, then efforts to dismantle or transform the regime must address those practices and relations. In uncovering the omnipresence of power, the fact that anything can be seen as a target of power, Foucault points the way toward new loci of resistance. Again, the body, for example, and discourses such as anorexia, can be seen respectively as the effect of power and as a locus of resistance.

Foucauldian analysis can be, and indeed, has been, made use of in spheres he did not even consider. It is, for example, made use of in feminist critiques of the art canon. Utilizing Foucauldian genealogy, feminists have exposed "the canon" as a product of male-dominated power. Noticing the absence of women in the canon has led art historians such as Linda Nochlin and Griselda Pollack to redescribe the history of art as the product of power relations. This in turn opens up new possibilities for art historians, art critics, artists, and audiences, and affects our very understanding of aesthetics. It makes our traditional understanding of art and art history vulnerable to the gaze of the Other. But it is important to note that Foucauldian analysis is a tool for, but not the catalyst of, such critique. *First* one notices that the interests/images/discourses of one's community, in this case the community of women, is absent.

If, then, Foucault meant to be doing no more than offering a tool for those engaged in oppositional struggles, a tool which could be amended to fit certain situations (interpretations), put aside when the circumstances do not call for it, or be thrown away when it becomes useless or obsolete—if *this* was his goal, then he was, at least to a large extent, successful and remains useful.

However, he failed in his goal insofar as he can also be said to participate in the patriarchal, colonizing, order. Given Foucault's analysis of the subject as the effect of power, the possibility for self-consciousness remains problematic. And since he placed the formation of self-identity within the disciplinary and normalizing structure of power, it is doubtful that such reflection, even if possible, would result in resistance.

Despite his opening up the political space, and freeing "us" to ask correspondingly new and provoking questions of it, he never adequately opened up a space for this "questioning us." This, despite his active role in prison reform and gay liberation. Though he did indeed work to help dissonant communities resist or revolt, the possibility of this community formation is significantly absent from his theory. He did not explain where the self-conscious voice of the Other could come from or how it could speak or assert itself for the purposes of resistance. I suggest that this failure is at least partially explained by his deemphasis on the importance of community for the formation of the subject of resistance.

At its worst, Foucault's poststructuralism keeps him from allowing for subjects sufficiently coherent to form communities of active resistance and transformation. At best it could be argued that while he did not exclude the possibility of the formation of community, neither did he take into account the seminal role of self-disclosure in community and community formation for the possibility of oppositional politics.

For various reasons, then, all the proponents of poststructural and postmodern politics I have been examining fail to provide a viable politics for oppositional struggles. It is time to assess this failure and its implications for an oppositional politics.

4

Evaluating "Post-Philosophies" for Oppositional Politics Selves, Community, and the Politics of Difference

For those who have been marginalized by the reign of reason—a reign which has ruled at least since Plato—postmodern critique can be liberating. It lays bare the artifice of all grand narratives and so frees us to create our individual and collective lives, to articulate our own voices, to diffuse the "Other" into just one more other.

Or does it?

My discussion of Foucault has raised serious doubts about the possibility of such freedom. If the very tools of critique and self-creation are themselves always formed within the power structures endemic to a particular time, place, culture, history, then how *can* we give "style" to our lives which is not simply one more effect of normalization and which is not simply the style made available (or allowed) by a capitalist, racist, patriarchal regime? And even ignoring this question, there remains the question of the usefulness of a theory which refuses self-identification. This amounts to no less than the question of whether or not empowerment is possible in a postmodern world built upon the precepts of a poststructuralism which insists everywhere on difference and the illegitimacy of a subject position. To answer this we must reconsider both the benefits and the dangers inherent in poststructuralist and postmodern theory. We must ask whether difference and empowerment are mutually exclusive—as they have been presented— or whether they can be combined to serve oppositional politics.

The law of difference

The metaphysical and ontological commitment to the law of difference (the inescapability of difference and the need for its recognition) generated by poststructuralist critique and presupposed in postmodern theory suggests a framework for evaluating politics: for a political theory to be viable, it must allow for the expression of difference. And in implying the creative and essentially political nature of structure it further suggests that empowering marginalized voices is possible: those concerns kept out of political debate can be made political by using techniques suggested by poststructuralism—techniques such as genealogy or deconstruction. All this is called into question, however, by the equation of unity with terror, for this does not allow identity formations necessary to political resistance. For this reason, the framework I am suggesting goes beyond what would be allowed in traditional accounts of poststructuralism, accounts given for example by Derrida, Althusser and the theorists I have explored above. I insist that we must not equate the law of difference with the demand to universalize difference, for the latter demands that we foreclose on the possibility of the subject, be it individual or communal. Though we understand identity as provisional, this provisionality need not deny the legitimacy of self- and communal identifications.

Borrowing from the poststructuralist account of difference, I suggest we accept the idea that all structure is temporary and even artificial, and is always open to the possibility of being redescribed. However, having thus understood "structure," I nevertheless insist, as "post-philosophies" do not, that any viable political theory necessitates structure—in particular it necessitates the need for the generation of subjects (or what I call "subjects-in-community," suggesting that there are no autonomous or non-plural subjects) and communities—even if these are themselves plural, internally inconsistent, open ended, and always amenable to deconstruction. Because poststructuralism as articulated by Derrida, Althusser, and either articulated or presupposed by Lyotard, Rorty, and Foucault, universalize difference, and because such universalization of difference (the rule of what I am calling the law of difference) precludes any formation of subjects and community, I conclude that poststructuralism, and postmodernism, which relies on the metaphysical and ontological commitments of poststructuralism, can be used, but not adopted wholesale for the purposes of oppositional politics. This conclusion follows from my disavowal of the coherence or possibility of a project which would universalize difference. This does not, however, mean that I disavow the importance of expressing the differences each one of us and our communities are. Such radical pluralism is essential to oppositional politics.[1] Equally essential, however, is the expression of similarity and the solidarity—even if temporary and partial—engendered by the realization of such similarities.

In my introduction to the chapter on Lyotard I showed how the poststructuralist critique of language forces the recognition of the inescapability of difference. A sign is fundamentally expressive of difference: the meaning of a signifier lies not in a relation of representation, as a word to a thing, but in its difference from other signifiers. This means that difference itself is never determinate or determinable. There is no system within which elements of difference are systematically structured. Rather, elements always generate new structures which fall outside of any ostensible system; the "Other" of poststructuralism marks this fact.

The subject is expressive of difference since it is constructed on, and as, language. Attending to the law of difference, I conclude with poststructuralism that human nature is always altered in creative ways. But this means that any structure—be it humanity, the subject, the social or cultural system, or history—comes into conflict with the law of difference because structure, traditionally understood, presumes to provide closure and coherence, unity or totality. Difference is repressed by structure. The question is whether or not this repression is terroristic.

I suggest that it is not in itself terroristic. Because it is of the very nature of language to creates structures, the repression of difference is the fact beyond which we can never get. The challenge is to envision a political theory or way of living which pays attention to this fact. One way of stating this challenge and dealing with the fact that all structure belies difference is to "give style to one's life." Another is to participate in a politics of difference which would, among other things, operate with the idea that all structures and all community relations are plural and subject to redescription. It would insist on describing phenomena from a multiplicity of perspectives, eschewing all hierarchies (and of course giving style to one's life and participating in a politics of difference are not incompatible projects).

One's political response to the law of difference can either be to give up on structure, this is what Lyotard and Foucault do when they are being consistent with their poststructuralist program, or we can do as I suggest: use the fact of difference to rethink our idea of structure. Let me provisionally call what I am proposing a "poststructuralist" or protean (as opposed to poststructuralist) understanding of structure. This reconceiving of structure gives up on the possibility of discerning essences or of identifying structures which are timeless or unchanging. It also conceives of all structure as being open to redescription and to deconstruction. This is not something philosophers or political theorists or anyone need worry about—it is simply the way things (all of

which are subject to the law of difference) are. This protean understanding of structure should not result in the giving up on structure,
for structure is something we linguistic beings cannot do without.
Without some kind of structuring, thought would not even be possible.
This is simply the logic of thought. This does not, however, mean that
structure must be understood as being "out there." On the contrary,
structures are created and always open to new creative interpretations.

The entities I am most concerned to reconceptualize along these
protean lines are subjects and community. The consequences of such
a rethinking will be taken up at the end of this chapter. But first I
wish to look one last time at the consequences of the political response
which conceives of poststructuralism as demanding the universalization of difference. I argue that this has the consequence of making
poststructuralism—and postmodern critique, which presupposes
poststructuralism—inimical to political action.

Refusing poststructural politics

Within the terms of the poststructuralist critiques I have considered
in the preceding chapters, totalization and totalitarianism are taken
as synonymous: the desire for the determination of difference, for
structure, is viewed exclusively as an instrument of repression, particularly of the creative (and potentially political) process by which a
given structure is generated. The poststructuralist concept of language
understood as a differential system of signs is thus suffused with political implications: it calls for resistance to oppression which it associates
with any determination or structuring of difference. Poststructuralism,
then, gets politicized in its concern with the deconstruction of otherness
into difference. All pretention to "normal" discourse, for example,
can be deconstructed to show that "normalcy" suppresses difference:
that it is also what it is not, is suppressed in determining what it is.
Structure both creates and excludes otherness.

In political terms, from the standpoint of postmodern analysis this
means that all second-order discourse (theories, legitimations) come
about by the silencing of other, no less "valid," voices. Language,
then, is never merely discursive;[2] it is also always political in that it
forces a choice between narratives, a choice which cannot be legitimated in any absolute sense, and which, though it may have a pragmatic defense, can always be redescribed to reveal a terroristic suppres-
sion of alternative narrative constructions.

And here the key is the category "legitimation" and "terror." I would suggest that what I have just been arguing loosely characterizes the poststructuralist/political commitments of Lyotard, Rorty, and Foucault. They each in their own way struggle with the belief that structure is suspect because it cannot be legitimated, and with the idea that structure imposes terror. I have shown how the problems with the political program of each can be traced back to these beliefs and ideas. But I have also suggested that their theories contain vestiges of the old paradigm they pretend to give up. There is no legitimation in the sense of an appeal to something absolute. But this does not mean— as Rorty notes in his better moments—that there are not pragmatic uses of legitimation, uses which cannot themselves satisfy the requirements of Rationality of Justice; uses which are themselves not legitimate in any absolute sense. Furthermore, the logic of difference necessitates the fact that no given structure will ever be able to range over all possibilities. Something will always be excluded, but exclusion is not necessarily terroristic; if we take poststructuralism seriously, it is simply how language operates.

So, while I agree that any and all structures can be deconstructed and reshaped, I do not agree that we have to view structure as being hopelessly unjust or terroristic. To view it this way is to hold on to the notion that there is something beyond difference or plurality. I will argue in the following sections that difference can accommodate unity (structure) so long as unity recognizes its subservience to difference. The idea that any structure or unity is necessarily subject to redescription is also politically attractive because it renders problematic all claims to sovereignty and hierarchy; it encourages the proliferation of political and creative voices and so is the best catalyst for "demarginalization" oppositional politics has (I put demarginalization in quotes because, of course, in the process of demarginalizing or forming the voice of "otherness," some other possibility is left—and sometimes created—at the margins).

When the law of difference is read as the destructuring of all structures and as demanding the delegitimizing of any and all claims to legitimation, the poststructuralist view of language as a differential system of signs overlaps with the political space of postmodernism. Both become a threat to oppositional politics because both insist always and everywhere on delegitimizing and destructuring. When read as a universal principle, the law of difference forecloses on the possibility of revitalizing the discourses of otherness, and so forecloses on the possibility of voicing marginalized concerns. But it is just such voicing that is the concern of oppositional politics. Insofar as poststructuralism and postmodernism universalize difference they are antithetical to oppositional politics.

Oppositional politics must first of all demand that it be allowed to address concerns of the Other. There are systematic structures, systematic political structures, actually in place which both create and marginalize otherness.[3] Oppositional politics cannot allow the law of difference to mask this fact. When it does, it becomes at best another useless theory having no practical application or even reality, and at worst it itself becomes implicated in the process of terrorism. The fact of "terrorism" creates the need for a political theory which could empower those who have been marginalized by normalizing discourse and the disciplinary power regimes.

Although my arguments have shown that poststructuralism and postmodernism do not themselves succeed in providing oppositional struggles with an adequate political theory and that they can at times even be shown to be part of the problem, I want to argue too that they can and must be mined for the purposes of oppositional politics.

Making use of poststructural and postmodern analysis

> Without community there is no liberation, only the most vulnerable and temporary armistice between an individual and her oppression. But community must not mean a shedding of our differences, not the pathetic pretense that these differences do not exist. (Lorde, *Sister Outsider*)

The question of empowerment is the other side of the question of how to give style to one's life which is not simply one more effect of the process of normalization. How, given that otherness is both marginalized by and constructed within normalizing power regimes, can the Other become empowered? How is oppositional politics possible?

I believe that poststructural analysis can be used to provide us with an answer, though my use of poststructuralism differs from that of Lyotard, Rorty, and Foucault. In particular, it differs in my using it to emphasize the importance of subjects-in-community and to recognize that the law of difference need not imply the *universalization* of difference.

In positing language (and not merely "linguistic" language—I have in mind written and pictorial texts as well) as a system of differences, poststructuralism enables us to claim that subjects are never hostage to the effects of a single narrative or power regime. Since power can come from as many points as there are possible narrative constructions, and since the law of difference teaches that redescription is always possible, the points of power and resistance are always at least *potentially* infinite.

This radical pluralism, inherent in the perspectivism engendered by the poststructuralist theory of the law of difference, makes poststructuralism and its critique of difference a rich resource for developing alternatives to the concepts of subjectivity, identity, resistance, and domination. Because it insists on the recognition of difference, it displaces the hierarchical opposition that characterizes capitalist patriarchal societies. This means that power can (at least theoretically) belong to those located at the margins as well as to those positioned in fields of dominance.

What I want to stress in thinking about the possibility of resistance, given the dominance of a particular normalizing and disciplinary discourse, is a further insight I take from poststructuralism—one which has been overlooked or underplayed in Lyotard's dilemma of how to present the "unpresentable," in Rorty's Romantic notion of the ironist, and in the dilemma I posed to Foucault, i.e., that of how, given the implications of power/knowledge for the subjection of the subject, it could be possible to build a theory of resistance. I have in mind the poststructuralist understanding of the subject: the subject which is a *linguistic subject* is always already a cultural construct. This is equivalent to claiming that subjects are always the effect and perpetuator of some community or other. This, in conjunction with the potentially open nature of language, is the key to creativity and empowerment—the key, in other words, to oppositional politics.

In asserting the usefulness of my adaptation of poststructuralism and postmodernism for oppositional politics, I wish to highlight three related claims: first, the law of difference means that the possible narrative constructions or stories we can tell about ourselves, the world, and others, are always open to redescription; second, the self is never the culmination of a single, or even necessarily coherent narrative; and third, the tools of narrative are not the property of an individual, but the product of history, culture, and community, which are themselves not monolithic entities. Resistance is never the property of an autonomous subject.

I have argued that poststructuralism and its law of difference, which postmodernism also adheres to, can be problematic for oppositional politics. To summarize: the danger lies in reading the law of difference as demanding the *universalization* of difference, as demanding the deconstruction of any and all centers including the deconstruction of a unified, coherent subject. This is sometimes joyfully described as the Nietzschean or aesthetic view of the self. However, such an aesthetic view of the self and its world is problematic for the purposes of empowerment. There may be no absolute grounding for the claims of science or morality. Nevertheless, the claims of modern science and the bourgeois discourse of justice are already in place; they shape and delimit both our public and private discourses. If oppositional politics is deprived not only of the legitimacy of appeal, but of the possibility of coherent resistance and of coherent *subjects* or loci of resistance, then the rule of racism and patriarchy has in effect, even if not in intent, been secured. This has the effect of leaving things as they are: those whose interests and voices are marginalized by the prevailing social, economic, and cultural order remain disempowered. Thus, if poststructuralism or postmodernism excludes the possibility of coherent subjects—and I claim one way of excluding coherent subjects is to exclude the possibility of community—neither could serve in building a useful political theory.

We must not allow the poststructural critique of language and the postmodern adoption of the law of difference to force us to conclude, as have some of its proponents, that there is no subject. In fact, my claim is that poststructuralism can be read—or *adapted* to read—as necessitating only the claim that there is no autonomous, wholly self-creating, or coherent *in the sense of single-minded or one-track* self. The self can be many subjects. But this does not mean that those subjects are, as they become in the analysis of Deleuze and Guattari, schizophrenic—if they were they would be unpresentable, unknowable, and unthinkable.

By the following formulation I want to suggest both my repudiation of the poststructuralist demand for the universalization of difference and my solution to the political problems it engenders: unity (the requirement that a thing be at least minimally coherent enough to be identified and redescribed) does not necessitate "unicity" (the demand that we speak with one voice). This is to claim that coherency does not necessitate speaking with one voice, that instability does not necessarily result in incoherence.

Nor does it mean that if radical pluralism is the mark of the self there can be no communities. Just as the self is a product of plural narratives, so too, "community" is always subject to deconstruction. And the subject which is a product of one community will also be a product of many others, not all of whose interests are compatible. However, we have vocabularies (though not only one vocabulary) only as a member of *some community or other*, and so *it is only as a member of some community or other that we are empowered*.

What Lyotard, Rorty, and Foucault fail to note, and what makes their version of postmodernism or poststructuralism ultimately unsatisfying for the purposes of the formation of voices of resistance, is that the possibility of resistance or the formation of oppositional discourses, the potential to create new "codes" and alternative "power regimes," the possibility of presenting what has been unpresented or speaking in new voices, is given with the extent to which we can come to identify with alternative communities, not all of which are equally articulate, or articulate in the same way. Empowerment is made possible (and this is where genealogical analysis *is* helpful) by realizing the extent to which we are never simply the member of a single community. In identifying ourselves as members also of marginalized communities we find the tools, i.e., the images and vocabularies, with which we can imagine a world other than the one suited to the interests of bourgeois liberalism. This can also be stated another way: the recognition that each one of us is radically plural makes alternative discourses an open possibility. The "unpresentable" is a fiction which marks the failure to take seriously the possibility of infinite redescriptions, redescriptions made possible by new community identifications.

One instructive example of empowerment through realigning one's perspective with alternative communities is given in the feminist redescription of the art canon. The breakthrough for women's art history and art criticism came when female art critics and historians switched their alliance from the community of male art historians and critics, whose canon is shaped from the standpoint of white privileged males and to which they belong by virtue of the fact that they are art historians and critics operating within the academy, to the community of women to which they also belong. Being both art critics and art historians, and women, are here being construed as different and incompatible narrative self-constructions (though for different purposes, they need not be described as incompatible). And of course, the community of women is also being broken down into the community of feminists, which on closer analysis could also be further deconstructed. But the point is, though the re-perspectivizing of the canon was not already in place, neither was the experience of women mute. The community of women had a language which could be appropriated (and selected from, since the "community of women" is not monolithic) for the purposes of rethinking the canon. When the shared knowledge women had from everyday encounters of being made into objects by the male gaze was included in their interpretations of the significance of artworks, a whole new dimension (need I say a political dimension) was given to art criticism. It now becomes less and less acceptable to discuss artists or artworks as a "thing apart." We can now ask not only "what is beauty," but "why?"

The same empowerment through realignment of preexisting, even if previously devalued, community identities continues in the community of feminists of color. Audre Lorde, bell hooks, Toni Morrison, Gloria Anzaldua, and others struggle with the creation of empowered identities, not just as women, but as black or Chicana women, as poor women, working women, lesbian or heterosexual women, educated or uneducated women. Each of these identities have needs and goals, and their combined needs and goals are not always compatible, even for the individual. But despite the fact that there is no single definitive answer of what it means to be a feminist or a woman of color or a person of color, the questions, questions which are formulated from the standpoint of community identifications, are being raised. And through the raising of these questions, new and powerful, even if unstable and incomplete, identities are being constructed. This challenging of the status quo comes from voicing those parts of the self not previously recognized or valued. The more different community alignments are explored, the more problems concerning identities and goals are discovered. Sure. But the process of resistance is begun; those community/identity interests are no longer silent. They too are made part of the debates about rights, justice, and respect, and they therefore open up new life possibilities. All from the starting point of subjects-in-community.

Thus the process of empowerment begins from the experience of a community already in place, even if this community itself can be further deconstructed ("Before I identified myself with the experience of being Black, but I realize I must also address my interests as a woman and these are not always compatible." "As a poor woman I have interests the feminist community is not meeting"), and even if the character of this community will change. Indeed, it is the potential redescription and even deconstruction of any community, along with the heterogeneous subject-communities which make up the self, that gives us the basis upon which an oppositional politics can be built—a politics where difference rather than hierarchy, heteronomy rather than homogeneity, and protean rather than disciplinary and normalizing discourse, is the goal.

Oppositional politics as I conceive of it appropriates the law of difference to keep before it the fact that any unity can always be deconstructed. "Women's issues," can be further deconstructed into class, or race, or cultural, or age, or sexual, or ablest issues (to name just a few of the sub-communities to which women's issues can be subdivided).

Certainly differences must be recognized. But this does not mean that difference has to begin as it does for Lyotard, from the view from nowhere, and indeed, if it had to begin from such a perspective it could never become empowered. There is no "view from nowhere"; every view is the viewpoint of some formed or forming vocabulary, a vocabulary which is both the product and effect of some community. And since any community is subject to re-perspectivizing and deconstruction, every vocabulary is malleable and hence potentially powerful. Empowerment, then, comes about as the result of the struggle of subjects-in-community.

This leads me to restate and emphasize the bad side of poststructuralism. Poststructuralist critique can be read in one of two ways. Its theory of difference which makes subjects radically plural guarantees the possibility of alternative discourses. In this, it provides us with the necessary foundation for any acceptable model of politics, "acceptable" being understood as allowing for the accommodation of difference and the recognition of the ineliminability of radical plurality. And on this point the poststructuralist is not necessarily postmodern: there is a human condition; the human condition is that the human condition can never be fully articulated; there is no single description of the human condition ranging over all of its possibilities. This is not, however, to render us impotent or speechless.

However, when universalized, the law of difference can also be used to preclude the possibility of politics—oppositional or otherwise. This happens when closure or unity is *equated* with terror. Such an equation renders us both impotent and speechless (impotent because speechless). Difference must not be erased—indeed it *cannot* be erased—but neither can it, nor should it, always be our guiding principle. We must be wary of difference becoming the grand narrative of the postmodern age.

When the subject is characterized, as I think it is in Lyotard's pagan attitude, in Rorty's ironic moments, and in Foucault's disavowals of the subject, as being entirely the mark of difference, the postmodernist loses the political game. Politics is not, and cannot be, modeled on schizophrenic, disconnected discourses (I cannot say "subjects") fighting both internally and externally. Such an extreme version of difference defeats its own purpose—far from giving voice to the marginalized Other, it deprives that Other of any meaningful language. It is no accident that postmodern theorists are notoriously difficult to read, to make sense of, their theories so difficult to articulate. One cannot at the same moment speak difference and speak coherently.

I have therefore been suggesting that we can pay attention to difference and speak as a unified subject, even while denying that unity entails or suggests unicity. We must not allow the universalization of totality, but we must also not accept the universalization of difference. All political exchange involves closure insofar as it demands subjects arguing for certain positions. However, this does not militate against difference if closure is reconceptualized along "poststructuralist" lines to mean it is necessarily temporary, subject to change, and only a partial description both of the interests of the agents of struggle, and of potential political interests in general. Only if "closure" is thus conceptualized and accepted can there be a *politics* of difference—and, as I shall argue, the position of a politics of difference thus conceived is a necessary (though not sufficient) requirement for oppositional politics. Neither the universalization of difference, nor the universalization of totality is a politically viable option for a *politics* of difference, or for a politics of opposition.

What are we looking for in a politics of difference? As I see it, the goal of a politics of difference is first of all to encourage self-respect and self-knowledge among individuals whose identity has either been silenced, devalued, or erased altogether because they belong to some group whose value is denied by the ideology of the controlling social powers. Once this is accomplished, that person can work as a member of various communities to insert her or his needs within the larger social structure, disrupting the complacency of the existing social and political "we."

But this raises some very important questions, among them the question of what would happen to difference in the ideal political state. Would the "we" simply become all-inclusive? Would there then be no more conflict between identity interests? Is there a common humanity beyond difference, or is a "common humanity" always evoked at the expense of difference? Does a politics of difference simply result in an ongoing battle over who determines and controls social and political interest? This was the kind of fear motivating white resistance to the black civil rights movement. If blacks were given the vote and with the vote could gain political power, the fear expressed by certain whites was that their interests would be jeopardized. Issues of justice were then perverted into a matter of protecting the existing power regime. From this standpoint a politics of difference threatens only to exchange one power regime for another.

Many "post-philosophers," Lyotard and Foucault included, are in agreement with the expectation that attention to difference makes politics an ongoing battle over power; only instead of fearing this result they actively encourage it. For them the law of difference militates against the ideal of social difference without exclusion. And since difference is the fact beyond which we cannot get, politics must be a matter of agonistics. In their view, a non-embattled state would not have solved the problems of conflicting interests brought on by the recognition of difference; it would merely have succeeded in imposing terror to artificially silence difference. The goal of a politics of difference on this model is to make sure differences are spoken and battled continually. In the words of Foucault: "Politics is only war continued by other means."

After the Los Angeles riots in 1992, Charlene Hunter Galt did a series on "The MacNeil/Lehrer News Hour" centered around the question, "Can we all get along?" This is, I think, a pressing question for a politics of difference. But in one respect, from the standpoint of oppositional politics, from the standpoint of those groups or individuals whose interests and needs are not being met in a white patriarchal society, debating the question simply prolongs their agony. Meanwhile, and despite the difficulties raised by Galt's question, socially and politically marginalized groups need to continue to construct their voice and to fight for power. But to do this these individuals and groups must first learn to value their differences. This must happen before political strategies and demands can be formulated (or perhaps both will happen simultaneously). To value ourselves we must learn to recognize the different identities that exist not just in society at large, but in each one of us as well. And, as I have argued, recognizing oneself in a variety of communities plays a large part in the process of self-identification and in the process of empowerment. Community identification is necessary to self-identification, and both are necessary to any politics of difference.

Given this assertion, it is beneficial to look at the critique of community in Iris Young's formulation of a politics of difference. Although

Young gives us one of the most complete and articulate formulations of a politics of difference, her political theory suffers from accepting what I believe to be the false dichotomy imposed by postmodern politics: either similarity or difference. Because of this she takes her commitment to difference to force the repudiation of community (along grounds similar to Lyotard's view of terror). In my view a politics of difference sensitive to the identity formation of marginalized individuals and working for their resistance must reconceive structure, including that structure which constitutes the self and community, to accommodate both difference *and* similarity.

Selves, community, and the politics of difference

According to Young, the ideal of community participates in a metaphysics (the metaphysics of presence, or the logic of identity) that denies difference:[4]

> [The ideal of community] presumes subjects that understand one another as they understand themselves. It thus denies difference between subjects. The desire for community relies on the same desire for social wholeness and identification that underlies racism and ethnic chauvinism on the one hand, and political sectarianism on the other.... [The ideal of community] thus provides no understanding of the move from here to there that would be rooted in an understanding of the contradictions and possibilities of existing society.[5]

Her critique of community accepts the totalizing effects of the law of difference. It assumes that members of a community see themselves as a non-conflicted, monadic unit, and that identification with others in the community can work only by erasing any differences between us. On Young's model, identification thus amounts to the demand "Be like me or disappear!"

No doubt we can and often do do this to one another—not only in communities, but in all kinds of conversations which presuppose understanding. How often has a friend been told of some momentous event only to interrupt with, "I know just what you mean. When I was married . . ."? Why not conclude that understanding only operates on a model of empathetic understanding which forces the silencing of experiences different from one's own?

But there is no reason to believe that community understanding or the recognition of similarity does foreclose on the recognition of genuine difference. So long as I recognize the many narratives I am I can also recognize that any story about another, or about myself, is necessarily incomplete.

Community identification is motivated by the desire to get clear on one or some of my identities (and recognizing myself in the experience of another may help me to do this) or to get clear on the larger social context in which that identity was formed (and community identification may also help me to do this). But that does not, as Young argues, mean that "any move to define an identity, *a closed totality* [emphasis mine], always depends on excluding some elements, separating the pure from the impure."[6]

The lesson to be learned from poststructuralism is that the logic of difference reveals the artificiality of any and all closure (structure). But this does not mean that we can do without closure or structure. We do not have to stop (nor can we stop) saying "I" or "us," even if we do have to be aware of the temporality of the meaning of that denotation. There is always more to those monikers than can be named at any one time precisely because our possibilities are always in excess of any named actuality.

Naming is only "terroristic" when the speaker or spokesperson denies this fact and treats the contingent as an absolute. I may focus on a particular aspect of a community, for example, that we are all women suffering from the demands of beauty placed on us by a phallocentric culture, and forget for a moment that considerations of class differences would affect our responses, realigning community identifications. The first community identity only terrorizes or forecloses on the formation of the second if it forgets that each "I" is always and necessary multiple. It is only then that another voice is refused hearing.

Community formation does not have to presuppose, as Young claims it does, that particulars must be brought under universal essences. If we understand the "poststructuralist" lesson of the protean nature of closure, we need not accept the validity of any universal essence. While we might agree with Young that "any definition or category creates an inside/outside distinction,"[7] we need not forget the artificiality of that distinction. If we repudiate the "logic of identity" we do not have to make distinctions based on the justification implied in that logic. And though the logic of identity understands the subject as a self-identical unity, community identification need not operate with this model. It can recognize both that the "I" is plural and that other "I's" in the community are equally plural.

Young writes, "As I [*sic*] understand it, difference means the irreducible particularity of entities, which makes it impossible to reduce them to commonness or bring them to unity without remainder." If difference meant this, there could be no politics.

There is no politics without sameness and unity, even if that unity always has a remainder. If there were no sameness there would be no entity coherent enough to claim "I," nor would there be any basis for group identification. And Young is deeply committed to a politics which recognizes and respects difference.

Within her political system coalition replaces community as the locus of empowerment and opposition:

> In a Rainbow Coalition, each of the constituent groups affirms the presence of the others as well as the specificity of their experience and perspective on social issues. . . . Ideally, a Rainbow Coalition affirms the presence and supports the claims of each of the oppressed groups or political movements constituting it, and arrives at a political program not by voicing some "principles of unity" that hide difference, but rather by allowing each constituency to analyze economic and social issues from the perspective of its experience. This implies that each group maintains significant autonomy, and requires provision for group representation."[8]

I don't see how this ideal of coalition escapes the concerns expressed by her critique of community, nor do I see why communities cannot or do not operate like a coalition. First, each coalition is made up of separate groups, and each group has an identity. Where do they get this identity if not by coming together as a community drawn together by similar interests, needs, or in other words, by similar (partial) identities? So within each coalition there "lurks" the specter of identity and community. Second, at the level of the larger coalition, identity formation seems inoffensive to Young because the identity is able to form a solidarity (even if tenuous and temporary) while recognizing difference. But if we understand selves and communities as necessarily complex, incomplete, and changing, there is no reason this description of coalition formation cannot also be applied to community formation. And third, in her critique of community Young is troubled by the fact that any identity denies difference. But this same "fact" must be applied to coalition building as well. It would be just as impossible for a political program growing out of a coalition to represent all of its voices as it would be for a person to represent all of her interests at any one time or a community to speak all of its voices at any one time.[9] To deny this would simply be to reassert the logic of identity at another level.

Young goes to great lengths in her critique of community to emphasize the artificial and temporary nature of all closure so that difference can be protected. But she should also acknowledge that politics necessitates the formation of identities—even if they always have a remainder and are never completely satisfactory statements of all the possible or important identity interests. A Rainbow Coalition cannot escape this fact any more than any other identity or group can. Her belief that it can represents her inability to bridge the gap between difference and unity and also represents her recognition that any politics, even a politics of difference, has to allow for unity.

What elevates a politics of difference over other political models (including traditional communitarian models) is its recognition of the metaphysics of difference even while claiming unity, or the acknowledgment that all unities necessarily have a remainder. It is in fact this remainder that encourages the hope that the future can always be different from, and perhaps even better than, the past.

A politics of difference

There are then both positive and negative aspects to the law of difference, and so, both positive and negative aspects to poststructuralism and postmodernism—or rather, whether or not these "post-philosophies" are of use for oppositional politics is a matter of how they are understood.

On the positive side, the law of difference forces politics to give up its exclusivity; it must construct itself with the voices of "otherness." This means that those whose concerns have traditionally been silenced or devalued can begin to assert their voice. The hope is that these newly heard voices will become available as cultural currency and so will be available as tools for shaping new ways of thinking about ourselves and our relation to others and the world and will become useful as tools for the implementation of new ways of being and acting.

There is nothing in itself good, or progressive about the possibility of change. What makes poststructuralist politics with its law of difference attractive is that there are many whose self-images, whose goals, interests, and desires, are not addressed within the white, capitalist, patriarchal power regime. Feminists, for example, are no longer willing to accept the public/private split. They demand that the private be politicized. Only then will women's voices be effective. From the perspective of the Other, then, radical change is necessary, and because the politics of difference entails this radical pluralism, it is attractive to oppositional politics.

In making us aware of the artificiality of closure, the law of difference makes politics radically plural, and this can make us more sensitive to, and tolerant of, difference. Even more so if we come to view closures about ourselves as likewise artificial or temporary; each one of us too participates in many different communities.

The problem with the law of difference as I have stated it is that taken to the extreme (treated as a universal principle), as it is in some present formulations of a politics of difference, it has the unintended consequence of excluding the possibility of oppositional politics.[10] The politics of difference must be reconceptualized to accommodate the fact that if any and all closures are terroristic, then the Other will never be given a chance to form itself as a political force. It will remain unpresented and unpresentable. And since, in fact, political systems (power regimes) which exclude or marginalize otherness do exist, then insofar as the law of difference can be used to keep the Other from articulating itself as a coherent, even if contingent identity, the law of difference serves the dominant and dominating order. It becomes a tool of colonization and keeps the Other defenseless.

I have been arguing that the postmodern repudiation of all grand narratives, where this is equivalent to disallowing all closure, is unacceptable from the position of those involved in oppositional struggles. Postmodern politics is *not* a viable option on this description for it repudiates the formation of community and of coherent subjects, both of which are necessary to the identity formation of otherness.

As we have seen, some current formulations of a politics of difference, useful as they are in other respects, are nevertheless marred by their equation of unity with the denial of difference. Young's, for example, would basically accept Lyotard's equation of all closures—of unity, consensus, and community—with terror. I have argued that this formulation fails to provide an adequate political theory in part because it fails to conceive of the subject and community as necessarily fluid entities. On Young's description the ideal of community is rejected because she conceives of it as necessarily exhibiting the desire for unicity. This may be true of traditional models of community which subsume the plurality of individual wills under the rubric of the "general will," but would not be true of the "poststructuralist" ideal of community I am proposing. This latter ideal could argue that since any move to define an identity or a closed totality always depends both on excluding some element of oneself and/or someone else, communities are always open to realignments and disavowals. One always changes narrative and communal positions. Thus difference need not be denied, and though it may have to be momentarily repressed, such repression is not necessarily terroristic. It would only make sense to equate all repression of difference with terror if there existed the possibility for a discourse in which all differences could be presented. But understanding language as a differential sign system makes this impossible. So Young rejects self and community identification (even though she needs self-identities for her theory of coalition) because she wants to protect a politics of difference. I suggest she need not go this far if she rethought what is meant by the "self"; I suggest she needs to rethink it as subjects-in-community.

What ought to be demanded in a politics of difference is not that each person have a single set of coherent goals, interests, and desires, but that she be able to construct a narrative that allows her to identify with communities that supply a particular story about what those interests are.[11] I have offered as an example the feminist art historian who is able to resist normalized readings of artworks by realigning her community identifications. I have also pointed out in that example that her resisting voice comes from another community identification. She is an art historian and also a feminist, and in this example resistance to dominant power regimes is made possible through differently foregrounding community identifications.

None of this would be possible in Young's formation of a politics of difference.

Within the work of Lyotard, Rorty, Foucault, and within Young's formulation of a politics of difference, attention to difference forecloses on community. I have been arguing, however, that the choice is not either difference or unity at the expense of terror. The problem will take care of itself if we realize that this dichotomy presents us with a false dilemma, for there is no ideal community or subject which is not subject to deconstruction. If *this* is suppressed, then community or the ideal of a "normal subject" is indeed repressive. But it is repressive because it presents the subject and community to be something they are not.

A politics of difference does not then imagine that all conflict could be resolved. There will always be groups which are forced to the margins. What it hopes for, however, is the fluidity of positions of power; it hopes to encourage the proliferation of voices. Thus it hopes to encourage skepticism about closure, skepticism about the privilege and necessity of any particular community without denying the temporary necessity of closed positions. The latter is necessary for articulate speech, the former for the possibility of de-normalization. Both are necessary for the empowerment of otherness.

Oppositional politics; similarity *and* difference

I have argued above that coalitions ought not to be accepted by Young and others as significantly different in character from community formation insofar as each coalition is made up of different communities. Young's formulation of coalition does not accommodate the fact that we enter coalitions not as isolated monads or autonomous subjects, but as members of some community (or as members of many communities). It ignores the fact that the subject is always already positioned within one or another community, is always a subject-in-community. And this entails the recognition on the part of the individual that she or he has similar experiences, or values, or needs as someone else.

It occurs to me that when a politics of difference is formulated by theorists of color—I am thinking, for example, of bell hooks, Audre Lorde, and Cornel West—community identification is the starting point for the valuing of previously marginalized identity formations and is also the basis for oppositional resistance. I do not know what, if any, conclusions can be drawn from the "fact" that theorists such as Iris Young and Jana Sawicki, both of whom are white (though taking into account other identity formations, they may also be constructed as being excluded from positions of power: they are, after all, also both women), are complacent about jettisoning just that identity (community identity) that serves as the catalyst for a politics of difference for these black theorists. But it does, though, seem to me to be a striking and potentially important difference in their formulations of a politics of difference, and one that needs more thought.

I would agree with those theorists of a politics of difference who argue that the recognition of points of *similarity* is key to the formation of oppositional politics. The recognition of similarity with others is crucial in denying and recognizing the harmful political implications of the public/private split. It is the recognition of the similarity of my pain or oppression in someone else that allows me to deny the idiosyncratic nature of my experience, and to deny my guilt at being different from the "norm." Coming to this recognition, identifying a "personal" pain with a pain belonging to others, and the consequent recognition of the ideological nature of these pains, is what makes novels such as *The Bluest Eye*, or books such as *Shadow on a Tightrope: Writings by Women on Fat Oppression*, or *This Bridge Called My Back: Writings by Radical Women of Color*, so effective in voicing marginalized identities, raising consciousnesses, and galvanizing opposition. *The recognition of similarity and the possibility of solidarity wakes us from the stupefaction of normalizing and disciplinary discourse.* The fact that such similarities and solidarities are partial and perhaps temporary does not lessen their fundamental importance (Audre Lorde, for example, refuses to give up the importance of community identification for oppositional politics and valued identity formation even though any such identity is always complicated for her by the fact that she is a woman, black, lesbian, a mother, a victim of cancer, the lover of a white, Jewish woman, etc.).

In arguing against Rorty's depoliticizing of the private, I have argued the benefits of, and necessity for, politicizing difference for the purposes of demarginalization and the empowerment of otherness. This led me to argue the need for a commitment to some formulation of a politics of difference and also for a commitment to radical pluralism. The radical pluralism entailed by this politics of difference operates with an expanded sense of the political. It thereby politicizes social relations that liberal theory often marginalizes. Furthermore, it addresses diversity in order to reveal forms of domination frequently overlooked within traditional emancipatory theory. And lastly, it operates with a relational and dynamic model of identity, recognizing plurality both within and between subjects.

I have also shown that it is this third point which, when taken to the extreme, becomes problematic. The extreme position seeks to carry out the poststructuralist demand to universalize difference, and insofar as a politics of difference insists on *universalizing* difference, it too becomes problematic. I have suggested that equating the law of difference with the universalization of difference and the *repudiation* of all closure, rather than recognizing the *temporality* of closure, is symptomatic of the inability on the part of some present proponents of a politics of difference to escape from the traditional paradigm. I have shown this to be true of Lyotard. It is also true of Iris Young and Jana Sawicki's otherwise eloquent statements of a politics of difference: they accept the traditional communitarian formulation of community instead of reconceptualizing it along "poststructuralist" lines, and in remaining within the old paradigm they have not helped oppositional selves to be self-conscious about their identity formation. I have shown that universalizing difference leads in Young's formulation of a politics of difference to repudiate community and so to overlook the fact that subjects-in-community is the fact beyond which we can never get, even in coalitions. Because of this, Young's formulation of a politics of difference also has an inadequate notion of the subject, for the subject must be seen as being formed within communities—many communities and changing communities. So in effect, any notion of a politics of difference which accepts the postmodern/poststructuralist disjunction: *either* difference *or* similarity leaves no locus for politics: no community, no self, no viable political theory.

Goals such as liberation and oppositional identity formation need not remain an impossible ideal. But to achieve oppositional identities we must have some clue about how values and interests become open to change and renegotiation, some clue as to how we might establish positions which challenge the sovereignty of normalizing and disciplinary discourse. My suggestion is that for this similarities and solidarities are fundamental; the subject of oppositional struggle is subjects-in-community and not the subject in isolation; nor is it no subject at all.

Endnotes

Introduction

1. One can think of Hobbes or Locke, but even Aristotle's list of virtues and his consequent conception of the well-ordered society speak for classist, patriarchal, and racist values—and one need not start this tradition with Aristotle.

2. For a discussion of "possessive individualism," see C. B. Macpherson, *The Political Theory of Possessive Individualism* (London: Oxford University Press, 1962), p. 3 and throughout.

3. Jean-François Lyotard, *The Postmodern Condition: A Report On Knowledge*, pp. *xxiii–xxiv*. As quoted by Joseph Margolis in his "Redeeming Foucault," pp. 17–18 of the unpublished manuscript.

4. Foucault, *History of Sexuality, Vol. I: An Introduction*, translated by Robert Hurley (New York: Vintage/Random House, 1980), p. 94.

5. If we insist that the criteria of the ubiquitous nature of politics is a precondition of any genuinely radical pluralism and necessary to any adequate postmodern position, we must credit Deleuze and Guattari as serious modern theorists. Their insistence on the ubiquitous nature of politics is grounded in what they take to be the nature of language: there are no features of linguistics which do not also pertain to politics. For them it is not just the contents of language which is a reflection of ideologies or forms of power—the *form* of language, too, must be understood as a product of struggle and conflict (Deleuze and Guattari, *A Thousand Plateaus*, pp. 75–110 and *passim*).

1. Lyotard

1. See *Just Gaming*, p. 36, written as sets of interviews with Lyotard and Jean-Loup Thébaud and translated by Wlad Godzich (Minneapolis: The University of Minnesota Press, 1985).

    Hereafter I will refer to works of Lyotard both as cited in the body of the text and in the footnotes with the following abbreviations:

    D= The Differend: Phrases in Dispute, trans. Georges Van Den Abbeele (Minneapolis: The University Of Minnesota Press, 1988).

    Diac= Diacritics: A Review Of Contemporary Criticism, Volume 14, No.3

(Fall 1984), which devoted the entire issue to the work of Lyotard and contains Lyotard's "The Differend, the Referent, and the Proper Name," as well as an interview with Georges Van Den Abbeele.

JG= Just Gaming, with Jean-Loup Thébaud, trans. Wlad Godzich (Minneapolis: The University of Minnesota Press, 1980).

PMC= The PostModern Condition: A Report on Knowledge, trans. Geoff Bennington and Brian Massumi (Minneapolis: The University of Minnesota Press, 1979).

2. PMC, p. 15.

3. PMC, p. *xxv*.

4. I am indebted to Jonathan Culler's discussion of semiotics in his *The Pursuit of Signs: Semiotics, Literature, Deconstruction* (Ithaca, NY: Cornell University Press, 1981).

5. Ferdinand de Saussure, *Course In General Linguistics* (New York: McGraw-Hill, 1966), p. 120.

6. Ibid., p. 114.

7. For a discussion of the problem of participation, see R. E. Allen, "Participation and Predication in Plato's Middle Dialogues," in *Plato: A Collection of Critical Essays, Vol. I: Metaphysics and Epistemology*, Gregory Vlastos, ed. (Garden City, NY: Anchor Books) 1971.

8. Jacques Derrida, *Structure, Sign and Play in the Discourse of the Human Sciences*, reprinted in *Critical Theory Since 1965*, Hazard Adams and Leroy Searle, eds. (Tallahasee: University Press of Florida, 1986) p. 84

9. Ibid., p. 85.

10. Ibid., p. 91.

11. It is worth noting that we would be different but not better. The idea that we'd be better off is not given a place in this theory. This is very different from critical theory, which still clung to the notion of positive social change. Marcuse, for example, was concerned with making the administration of consciousness amenable to critique because he thought that in so doing society could be changed for the better—to better accord with our "real" interests, needs, desires.

12. *Language games*, the preferred term in *The Postmodern Condition*, is replaced in *The Differend* by the term *phrase regimens*. This replacement represents an advanced awareness (sophistication) in Lyotard's theory. He realized that the terminology of language games can be taken to suggest transcendental subjectivity—a subject which uses language, but exists at some point outside of it, determining its use. For Lyotard, however, the subject is always immanent in language. There are times when for convenience's sake I use "language games." The reader should be aware that in doing so no transcendent subject is implied.

    The Fall 1984 issue of *Diacritics* was devoted to Lyotard. In an interview given there he explains his switch from the term *language game* to *phrases* thusly:

    ... it seemed to me that "language game" implied players that made use of language like a tool box, thus repeating the constant arrogance of Western anthropocentrism. "Phrases" came to say that the so-called players were on the contrary situated by phrases in the universe, those phrases present, "before" any intention. Intention is itself a phrase, which doubles the phrase it inhabits, and which doubles or redoubles the addressor of that phrase" (Diac 17).

13. It follows from this argument that all objects whatsoever—not merely selves—are decentered.

14. The "unpresentable" are those possibilities which are not part of the received view, which haven't been co-opted by technocratic authority, and are thus expressions of our genuine possibilities.

15. To anticipate: the problem is that aesthetics cannot discriminate the just from the unjust (JG 90). Thus, his pagan model of justice, which is ruled by the aesthetic demand for multiplicity, must itself be constrained by a regulative Idea. This leads to difficulties with his erstwhile radical theory.

16. See Cecile Lindsay, "Experiments in Postmodern Dialogue," Diac pp. 52–64.

17. It should be noted that this makes Lyotard susceptible to the charge that he is subjecting all genres of discourse to the principle of success, to a universal principle of winning. He notes this himself, but does not address it. See D ¶185.

18. In the *Postmodern Condition* agonistics is a founding principle of Lyotard's theory of language games. His view is that all games depend on a feeling of success won at the expense of an adversary, and his theory of agonistics is dependent on the veracity of such a view.

But is all game playing a kind of fighting? Think of jump rope, paddycake, hide-and-seek, solitaire, make-believe. . . .

But even if his theory of agonistics fails to convince, he may still be correct in his view that paralogy and not consensus is the appropriate model for heteromorphous language systems. In other words, if language games are heteromorphous, subject to heterogeneous sets of pragmatic rules, then it may not be possible for all speakers to come to agreement on which rules or metaprescriptions are universally valid for language games. Furthermore, if consensus is a function of forcing conformity where diversity would be the rule, then there is good reason to make the goal of dialogue paralogy rather than consensus—for paralogy would aim at encouraging a proliferation of models of discussion rather than searching for a set of rules which would end it.

The commitment to paralogy over consensus also has its aesthetic counterpart: the artists are set to guard at the gates of discussion, to remind us that all that is possible to express can never be expressed, though it can—by means of terror—be forced to close, hence his thesis that since language games are necessarily heteromorphous, they can be united only at the expense of terror (PMC 81). The job of avant-garde art is to force us to keep forever before us the possibility of expressing more than has yet been expressed; they therefore keep the present "reality" in question. See for example PMC, pp. 78–80. (For more on consensus see PMC 60–61 and *passim*.) See also Lyotard's *The Inhuman: Reflections on Time*, Geoffrey Bennington and Rachel Bowlby, trans. (Stanford, CA: Stanford University Press, 1991) and my review of this book in *International Studies in Philosophy* (forthcoming).

19. However, as I shall argue, the Kantian Idea adopted by Lyotard does make use of such a notion of community. This is one of the reasons his Kantianism is unacceptable.

20. See also D, p. 140, ¶196.

21. Indeed, Lyotard sometimes writes as if community, along with consensus, is a terroristic imposition of unity on difference. But then what can be made of politics—especially since Lyotard is not advocating (as Deleuze, for example, might) anarchy? It should be noted that his thesis regarding the sovereignty of language games implies the legitimacy of localized communities. It should also be noted that this construction of community at any rate *does* replicate those things about community which a politics committed to expressing difference would abjure. The question once again is how to retain community necessary to a well-working politics and at the same time open the floor up to difference—or to the unpresentable.

22. These questions do not only set the stage for the remaining discussion of Lyotard, they are also the sorts of questions which concern me when considering the option offered by postmodern politics since one of the things which unites all versions of postmodern politics is the insistence that politics "must be the idea of multiplicity and diversity"—and at the simplest level, what the careful reader, even one sympathetic to the commitments of a politics of difference, must wonder is, "how?" And so these questions will not be left behind with this chapter.

23. Is his notion of sovereignty incompatible with his description of the linking of phrases as constituting a "victory" discussed above? To the victim who claims that she is not being allowed to be heard, the tribunal can reply "you may too be heard, but only in your own language, according to your own rules—or if you revise your complaint in such a way that it makes sense to us," in which case her claim might be so revised (co-opted) as to no longer be able to express *her* meaning. The concept of the differend argues for the expansion of language, the theory of the sovereignty of language games the isolation of language games. This marks an important conflict present in Lyotard's thought.

24. Nevertheless, the concept of justice as a multiplicity is itself illegitimately used as an absolute and not a relative term. This gets Lyotard into trouble when he tries to legitimate its absolute status.

25. This is a point I will come back to. For further discussion on this point see also: Seyla Benhabib, "Epistemologies of Postmodernism: A Rejoinder to Jean-François Lyotard," in *Feminism/Postmodernism*, ed. Linda Nicholson (New York: Routledge, 1990), pp. 107–30.

26. This is the problem with "language game" talk. It intimates that these games are clearly delineable, that the rules can be confined to a single game. It comes out of a philosophic expectation that each game could be analyzed into its parts without any remainder. But in fact each "game" is already plural, and this is a reflection of the ineliminable complexity of the social space and the social subject. While it may be true that words have their meaning as part of a context, that context cannot be confined to a single or particular set of rules. I think that we would do well to replace the Wittgensteinian talk of language games with the Deleuzeian concept of the rhizome. The model of language games has language divided into neat and self-sufficient components. The model of a rhizome sees it as being uncontainable, as a "deterritorialized flow" which "spreads like oil." See Gilles Deleuze and Felix Guattari, *A Thousand Plateaus: Capitalism and Schizophrenia* (Minneapolis: The University of Minnesota Press, 1987), pp. 1–25 and *passim*.

27. See his "Rephrasing the Political with Kant and Lyotard: From Aesthetic to Political Judgments," in Diac, pp. 72–90.

28. This is not only important, but also controversial. Lyotard often claims to be modeling his paganism after Kant's judgments of the sublime. But I believe he vacillates between allowing his paganism the freedom of Kant's aesthetic model and demanding the rigor of Kant's moral imperatives.

29. This would seem to entail the thesis that there can never be a locus of responsibility, we could never impute a just or unjust action to an *individual*. But then, for all his excursion into Kant, Lyotard is no better off than when he started. He still has not found a way of making normative judgments.

2. Rorty

1. I owe this formulation of the problem to my discussions with Roger King.

2. These articles appear in *The London Review of Books,* April 17, 1986; May 8, 1986; and July 24, 1986; respectively. They also appear in a revised version as the first three chapters of *Contingency, Irony, and Solidarity.* I will be making use of both.

    For the sake of simplicity, I will refer to these and other of Rorty's works in the body of the text with the following abbreviations:

    CL= "Contingency of Language"

    CS= "Contingency of Self"

    CC= "Contingency of Community"
    (The "contingency articles" first appeared in *The London Review Of Books,* CL: 17 April 1986, pp. 3–6; CS: 8 May 1986; pp. 11–15; and CC: 24 July 1986, pp. 10–14. A revised version also appears as the first three chapters in CIS.)

    CIS= *Contingency, Irony and Solidarity* (Cambridge: Cambridge University Press, 1989).

    PBL= "Postmodern Bourgeois Liberalism," *The Journal of Philosophy,80,* 1983, pp. 585–591.

    PDP= "Priority of Democracy to Philosophy," *The Virginia Statute for Religious Freedom*, Merrill D. Peterson and Robert C. Vaughn, eds. (Cambridge: Cambridge University Press, 1988), pp. 257–82.

    This does not represent all the texts of Rorty's to which I will refer, but only those most frequently quoted.

3. Thus "civilized" is equated with "patriarchal" and so , to deliberate close-mindedness (why, for example, does the civilized "man" not investigate other cultures, etc.?).

4. "Solidarity or Singularity? Richard Rorty between Romanticism and Technocracy," chapter 5 of her book *Unruly Practices: Power, Discourse, and Gender in Contemporary Social Theory,* (Minneapolis: University of Minnesota Press, 1989). I found my own reading of Rorty to be much in sympathy with her own and I

am much indebted to the clarity of her discussion. Future references to this book will be cited in the body of the text.

5. The first draft of my discussion of Rorty was confusing. It attempted to follow the contradictions in Rorty's arguments as these arguments are presented through-out the body of his recent works. This made for a confusing and thorny discussion (as indeed it does in the original). I am indebted to Nancy Fraser's article "Solidarity or Singularity" for suggesting a more coherent way to organize my discussion. In breaking up, as she does, Rorty's argument into the three separate discussions of his understanding of the relation between the ironists and liberalism, I am able to present him in the best light possible, and it also makes it easier for the reader to follow the arguments. I wish to note, however, that this is not the way Rorty presents his arguments; he all too often contradicts his thesis from one sentence to another. For a truer, albeit less coherent, discussion of Rorty, see my "Richard Rorty's Failed Politics," in *Social Epistemology* 7, no. 1 (1993), pp. 61–74. It should also, I suppose, be noted that while Frazer's article inspired the idea of how to more coherently organize my discussion, the content of that discussion is my own.

6. For an example of such critique see the work of Linda Nochlin and Griselda Pollock.

7. Richard King, "Self-Realization and Solidarity: Rorty and the Judging Self," in J. H. Smith and W. Kerrigan, eds., *Pragmatism's Freud: The Moral Disposition of Psychoanalysis* (Baltimore: Johns Hopkins University Press, 1986), p.38.
   Jitendra Mohanty has suggested to me—and I think this may in fact be a better formulation—that the reverse may be the case: because our private concerns and judgment have social origins and implications, there is no "one" without "two" or more.

8. Ibid., p. 44.

9. I am reminded yet again of Nietzsche here, whose insight and dilemma it was (an insight and dilemma which also haunts many formulations of postmodernism) that the self is always inscribed within the limits of language—the "consciousness" of a culture:

   My idea is . . . that consciousness does not really belong to man's individual existence but rather to his social or herd nature. . . . Consequently, given the best Will in the world to understand ourselves as individually as possible, "to know ourselves," each of us will always succeed in becoming conscious only of what is not individual but "average" (*The Gay Science*, trans. Walter Kaufmann [New York: Vintage/Random House, 1974] p. 354).

3. Foucault

1. "On my view, we should be more willing than we are to celebrate bourgeois capitalist society as the best polity actualized so far, while regretting that it is irrelevant to most of the problems of most of the population of the planet." Rorty, *Consequences of Pragmatism* (Minneapolis: University of Minnesota Press, 1982 p. 210)

2. For a provocative attempt to reconcile Foucault's thesis of power/knowledge with the possibility of resistance see Jana Sawicki, *Disciplining Foucault: Feminism Power and the Body* (New York: Routledge, 1991).

3. Richard Shusterman and Pierre Bourdieu have interesting discussions of the political nature of aesthetics. Shusterman for example argues that Rorty's supposedly politically neutral aesthetic vision in fact harbors the values of bourgeois liberalism:

> One does not need a very penetrating or subversive eye to see in Rorty's glorification and quest of the new, in his "aesthetic search for novel experience and novel language," precisely that old worship of the new which sustains and fuels the rapid and relentless pace of commodity consumption in our late-capitalist consumer society. . . . Rorty's quest to acquire more and more new experiences and vocabularies is the philosophical counterpart of the consumer's quest to maximize consumption, both are narcotic dreams of happiness induced by capitalism's master dream . . . of greater sales and greater profits" (Shusterman, "Postmodern Aestheticism," *Theory, Culture, and Society* 5, pp. 335–55).

For a more general and more extended discussion of the political nature of aesthetics, see Pierre Bourdieu's influential work: *Distinction: A Social Critique of the Judgement of Taste*, trans. Richard Nice (Cambridge: Harvard University Press, 1984).

4. PMC, pp. 77–82; JG, pp. 10–61.

5. This succinct way of splitting the difference between the concerns of poststructuralism and postmodernism was suggested to me by Joseph Margolis. In this regard I also found useful his unpublished manuscript, "Redeeming Foucault."

6. "Questions of Method," p. 116. Reprinted in *After Philosophy, End Or Transformation?*, Kenneth Baynes, James Bohman, and Thomas McCarthy, eds. (Cambridge: M.I.T. Press, 1987). Hereafter referred to as QM.

7. *Foucault Live (Interviews, 1966–84)*, trans. John Johnson, Sylvère Lotringer, ed., printed in the *Semiotext(e)* series (New York: Columbia University, 1989), p. 305. Hereafter referred to as FL.

8. FL, p. 312.

9. QM, p. 101. For a discussion of the relation between truth and power/knowledge see *Power/Knowledge: Selected Interviews and Other Writings*, Colin Gordon, ed. (New York: Pantheon, 1980) p. 93ff. Hereafter referred to as P/K.

10. QM, p. 104.

11. *After Philosophy*, p. 97.

12. P/K, pp. 93ff.

13. This point invites comparison with Nietzsche's *The Genealogy of Morals* #XII.

14. This perhaps is not so dissimilar to Rorty's argument that imaginative identification is the fundamental political tool. Is Foucault also implying here that the intellectual is the key to social hope? Could imagination be actively productive without genealogical analysis? Foucault is not clear on this. Though he obviously wants to make theory merely a tool of oppositional resistance, it is not clear how resistance could be effected—if indeed it can—without it. And even so, the question remains, just

how important is genealogy; is it more than the academic pastime of an intellectual? I will be returning to these sorts of questions.

15. *History of Sexuality, Volume I: An Introduction*, trans. Robert Hurley (New York: Vintage/Random House, 1980), p. 93. Hereafter referred to as HS.

16. Ibid.

17. HS, p. 93.

18. P/K, p. 114.

19. P/K, p. 119. See also Sandra Bartky's discussion of constitutive power in her article "Foucault, Femininity, and the Modernization of Patriarchal Power," in *Feminism and Foucault*, eds. Irene Diamond and Lee Quinby (Boston: Northeastern University Press,1988), pp. 61–80.

20. P/K, p. 59.

21. P/K, p. 74.

22. P/K, p. 98. The individual is at the same time the vehicle of power and the means through which power is articulated. If we want then to bring power under our active, rather than merely passive, control, we will have to become conscious of the effects of power. Foucault's contribution to the subversion of dominant power regimes is to offer genealogical analysis as a tool for the building of such consciousness.

23. HS, p. 94.

24. For more on the ubiquity of power, see P/K, pp. 141, 142, 189; and "The Subject and Power," printed as an afterword in Hubert L. Dreyfus and Paul Rabinow, *Michel Foucault: Beyond Structuralism and Hermeneutics* (Chicago: The University of Chicago Press, 1982), p. 222.

25. P/K, p. 85.

26. CIS, p. 63.

27. Ibid.

28. Ibid.

29. FL, p. 109.

20. Ibid., p. 191. Thus Foucault's understanding of truth as it relates to the ubiquity of power shares certain similarities with Lyotard: he too conceives of politics as "war carried on by other means," as an "agonistic relationship" which is "less of a face-to-face confrontation which paralyzes both sides than a permanent provocation."

31. CIS, p. 64.

32. Ibid., n24, p. 64.

33. *Language, Counter-Memory, Practice: Selected Essays and Interviews*, ed: Donald F. Bouchard (Ithaca, NY: Cornell University Press, 1977), p. 230. Hereafter referred to as LCMP.

34. CIS, p. 64.

35. Ibid., p. 63, n21.

36. Ibid.

37. Ibid., p. 63, n21.

38. LCMP, pp. 221–22.

39. Ibid., pp. 222 and 226.

40. Ibid., p. 228.

41. See, for example, *The History of Sexuality, Volume I.*

42. *The Foucault Reader*, ed. Paul Rabinow (New York: Pantheon, 1984), p. 386.

43. See CIS, p. 63, n21.

44. P/K, p. 133.

45. "It Is Really Important to Think," p. 134.

46. LCMP.

47. Richard Rorty, "Habermas and Lyotard on Postmodernity," *Praxis International* 4:32–44, p. 40ff.

48. Ibid.

49. The following is a paraphrase of Barry Smart's discussion of Foucault in "The Politics Of Truth," p. 167, found in *Foucault: A Critical Reader*, ed. David Couzens Hoy (Oxford: Basil Blackwell, 1986).

50. Ibid., p. 160 and *passim.*

51. Foucault, "Two Lectures" from *Power/Knowledge*, p. 81. Quoted in Barry Smart, p. 167. The other passages quoted from Smart are also taken from page 167.

52. Nancy Fraser, *Unruly Practices: Power, Discourse, and Gender in Contemporary Social Theory* (Minneapolis: The University of Minnesota Press, 1989), especially pp. 17–69; Richard Rorty, CIS, HL; "Foucault and Epistemology," in *Foucault: a Critical Reader*, pp. 41–50; Michael Walzer, "The Politics of Michel Foucault," ibid., pp. 51–68; Charles Taylor, "Foucault on Freedom and Truth," ibid., pp. 69, 102; Jürgen Habermas, "Taking Aim at the Present," ibid., pp. 102–8; and also Habermas's *The Philosophical Discourse of Modernity*, trans. Frederick Lawrence (Cambridge, Mass.: M.I.T. Press, 1987), pp. 265–93 and *passim.*

53. QM, pp. 113–14.

54. See Rorty's critique of Foucault: HL, pp. 40–41.

55. Nancy Fraser, "Foucault's Body Language: A Posthumanist Political Rhetoric?", op. cit., p. 56.

56. Fraser, ibid., p. 58.

57. Joseph Margolis, "Redeeming Foucault," p. 23.

58. Ibid., p. 23.

59. Ibid., p. 24

60. Ibid., p. 27.

61. CIS, p. 64, n24.

62. LCMP, p. 209.

63. P/K, p. 230.

64. LCMP, p. 208. Foucault argues in this passage that the "masses," and here I take the liberty of replacing "the masses" with "the repressed," know their situation

and are capable of expressing it. But then why is there the problem of marginalization and domination? Because the repressed operate within a system that doesn't recognize the validity of alternative voices. The task then is to break out of this system and form a new one in which those voices, those discourses and knowledges invalidated in previous regimes, would now be productive of the "true" discourses. The question which I will be addressing in the following section, however, is whether or not Foucault allows for the possibility of active and self-conscious transformation.

65. Ibid.

66. P/K, p. 145.

67. LCMP, p. 208.

68. FL, p. 199.

69. FL, p. 308.

70. QM, p. 112.

71. FL, p. 191.

72. QM, p. 114. Barry Smart argues a similar position. See "The Politics of Truth and the Problem of Hegemony," p. 167.

73. QM, p. 114.

74. QM, p. 115.

75. CIS 87.

76. Thus, Rorty imagines truth as the legitimate property of the ironist because he or she can choose what to view as true because he or she views nothing as true. But as Foucault points out in "Truth and Power," "truth isn't the privilege of those who succeeded in liberating themselves." In fact, truth "induces regular effects of power." (Quoted on page 108 in Mark Maslan's "Foucault and Pragmatism," *Raritan* 7 [Winter 1988], pp. 94–114. See Maslan for an extended Foucauldian critique of Rorty's notion of truth.)

77. CIS, p. 87.

78. P/K, p. 82.

79. FL, p. 293.

80. HS, pp. 95–96.

81. Nancy Hartsock, "Foucault on Power," in *Feminism/Postmodernism*, ed. Linda Nicholson (New York: Routledge, 1990), p. 167.

82. This question was suggested by my reading of Hartsock, even though I disagree with her assessment of Foucault.

83. Jane Flax makes a related point: "Since we live in a society in which men have more power over women it makes sense to assume that what is considered to be more worthy of praise may be those qualities associated with men. As feminists, we have the right to suspect that even praise of the female may be (at least in part) motivated by a wish to keep women in a restricted (and restrictive) place. Indeed, we need to search into all aspects of society (the feminist critique included) for the expressions and consequences of relations of domination." In other words, language is never *merely* discursive (see my note 92 below). Jane Flax, "Postmod-

ernism and Gender Relations in Feminist Theory," in *Feminism/Postmodernism*, pp. 55–56.

84. Susan Bordo, "Feminism, Postmodernism, and Gender Skepticism," ibid., p. 51.

85. Ibid.

86. FL, p. 189.

87. P/K, p. 88.

88. P/K, p. 98.

89. Sandra Lee Bartky, "Foucault, Femininity and the Modernization of Patriarchal Power," in *Feminism and Foucault: Reflections on Resistance,* Irene Diamond and Lee Quinby, eds. (Boston: Northeastern University Press, 1988), p. 82.

90. P/K, pp. 73–74.

91. FL, p. 313.

92. As Joseph Margolis points out, "the recovery of the 'other' requires a parasitic use of language that is never merely discursive, though it will appear to be." ("Redeeming Foucault," p. 21 of the unpublished manuscript.) It is never merely discursive because it is always recovered within a power structure which is expressive of relations of domination.

93. Jana Sawicki, "On Using Foucault for Feminism: A Personal Reflection," p. 2 of an unpublished article.

94. Ibid., p. 3.

95. FL, p. 252.

96. See Sandra Lee Bartky, p. 77 and *passim*. See also Foucault's biography of Herculine Barbin, a hermaphrodite. "Her" life is an example of the way in which a subject who refuses the "normal" gender distinctions is destroyed. Judith Butler is correct to note that "this question of being a woman is more difficult than it perhaps originally appeared, for we refer not only to women as a social category, but also as a felt sense of self," a culturally conditioned or constructed subjective identity. See Judith Butler, p. 324 in *Feminism/Postmodernism*. Her point, a point that I am arguing is Foucauldian, is true not only of women, but of Indians, Jews, African-Americans, etc.

97. P/K, p. 208.

98. Christine Di Stefano, "Dilemmas of Difference: Feminism, Modernity, and Postmodernism," in *Feminism/Postmodernism*, p. 76.

99. Ibid.

100. The privileging of the individual perpetuates, for example, the devaluation of voices that would speak from the standpoint of an ethics of care and compassion, or who would speak not from the standpoint of an isolated, appetitive individual, but from the standpoint of the community with which she or he allies her or himself. Carol Gilligan's research serves as an example of how "a different voice" gets silenced within patriarchal regimes. Her research on women's development shows that women tend to use a language of morality, which takes interrelatedness as a given, and in so doing arrives at an "understanding of life that reflects the limits of autonomy and control." See Carol Gilligan, *In a Different Voice* (Cambridge: Harvard University Press, 1982).

101. Judith Butler, op. cit., p. 326.

102. James Miller's autobiography has a fascinating argument to the effect that one can read the whole of Foucault's oeuvre as part of the Nietzschean quest to create oneself, and that for Foucault this quest resulted in a horrible sense of aloneness (as it did, I think for Nietzsche as well). Using Miller's discussion of Foucault's existential loneliness, one might be able to locate a psychological explanation for the contradictions found in Foucault's theory of the subject. See James Miller, *The Passion of Michel Foucault* (New York: Simon and Schuster, 1993).

103. Laurie Hicks, "A Feminist Analysis of Empowerment and Community in Art Education," Studies in Art Education Vol 32, no. 1 (Fall 1993) p. 43.

104. Op. cit., p. 327.

105. Nancy Hartsock, "Foucault On Power: A Theory For Women?" in *Feminism/ Postmodernism*, p. 163.

106. That such interpersonal discourse is essential for formulating oneself may, as Gilligan among others have noted, be an experience of the female alternative to male values—and one which may either already be in place for other marginalized groups, or a way of life others would value were they given the option. If this is the case, then excluding or devaluing such strategies is yet one more example of disempowerment of the dominant patriarchal regime.

107. Op. cit., pp. 13–14.

108. Mark Anderson, "Anorexia and Modernism, or How I Learned to Diet in All Directions," in *Discourse* 11, no. 1 (Fall-Winter 1988–89), p. 38.

109. And here I would take issue with Iris Marion Young and her rejection of the importance of community and the experience of "face-to-face encounters" for the formation of a politics of difference. See "The Ideal of Community and the Politics of Difference," in *Social Theory and Practice* (Spring 1988). pp. 1–26.

    In favor of my position of the importance of community, storytelling, and face-to-face encounters for the formation of oppositional self-identities and discourses, I refer the reader to the following: *Discourse*, Fall-Winter 1988–89; *Gender/Body/Knowledge*, a collection of essays edited by Susan Bordo and Alison Jaggar (New Brunswick, NJ: Rutgers University Press, 1986). Especially of interest in that collection is Bordo's article, "The Body and the Reproduction of Femininity: A Feminist Appropriation of Foucault"; *The Female Gaze*, edited by Lorraine Gamman and Margaret Marshment (Seattle: The Real Comet Press,1986); and Iris Marion Young's article, "On Throwing Like a Girl: A Phenomenology of Feminine Body Comportment, Motility, and Spatiality," in *The Thinking Muse: Feminism and Modern French Philosophy* (Bloomington: Indiana University Press, 1989).

4. Evaluating "Post-Philosophies" for Oppositional Politics

1. Radical pluralism must be differentiated from liberal pluralism. One of the salient differences I am presupposing here is that liberal pluralism thinks of competing interest groups as having relatively stable identities that compete on an equal basis for political representation. Radical pluralism denies the stability of group and of individual identity, that difference is the mark not only of individuals but also of

groups, and also denies that in a world in which oppression is a reality justice demands that all groups have an equal right to representation. For further discussion, especially on this last point, see Iris Marion Young's "Polity and Group Difference: A Critique of the Ideal of Universal Citizenship," Ethics 99 (January 1989), pp. 250–74.

2. This point was suggested to me in reading Margolis's *Redeeming Foucault.*

3. Many feminists and activists of color have remarked with no little suspicion on the politics of identity deconstruction. Isn't it suspicious, they ask, that just at the moment when marginalized groups are demanding their voice, the death of the author is heralded? Since there is, however, an identity of the author of most of our recognized values, and that author is white, male, and propertied, to deny the subject is to leave the status quo in place and unchallenged. Oppositional politics refuses to abandon this challenge.

4. Iris Marion Young, "The Ideal of Community and the Politics of Difference," *Social Theory and Practice* 12 (Spring 1986), p. 1.

5. Ibid., pp. 1–2.

6. Ibid., p. 7.

7. Ibid., p. 3.

8. Iris Marion Young, *Justice and the Politics of Difference* (Princeton, NJ: Princeton University Press, 1990), pp. 188–89, and *passim.*

9. I will return to my dissatisfaction with viewing coalitions as an advance over community in the following section.

10. In addition to Iris Young's theory, another clearly articulated and forceful theory of a politics is difference, though on my view one that is problematic for the same reasons Young's is, is given by Jana Sawicki in "Foucault and Feminism: Toward a Politics of Difference," *Hypatia* 1, no.2 (Fall 1986), pp. 1–3, and in her "Politics of Difference: Towards a Radical Pluralism, presented at the Third International Social Philosophy Conference, In Charlotte, N.C., June 4–6, 1987.

11. And sometimes we do this through face-to-face relationships, but not always. We can also identify with strangers as being part of our community. So long as we keep in mind that what we are identifying with is only a part of that stranger's set of identity interests, such an identification does not need to deny differences between myself and this other. The relationship between similarity and difference need not be a disjunctive one. For Young's critique of community on the grounds that it privileges face-to-face relations, thereby doing violence to difference, see "The Ideal of Community and the Politics of Difference," and *Justice and the Politics of Difference*, p. 232ff. Much of her criticism presupposes the traditional ideal of community, which I am suggesting can and needs to be reformulated.

Bibliography

Abbeele, Georges Van Den. "Up Against the Wall: The Stage of Judgement." *Diacritics* 3 (Fall 1984):90–99.

Adams, Hazard and Searle, Leroy, ed. *Critical theory since 1965*. Tallahassee: Florida State University Press, 1986.

Adorno, Theodor. "Society." *The Salmagundi Reader*, edited by Robert Boyers and Peggy Boyers. Bloomington: Indiana University Press, 1983.

Allen, Jeffner, and Young, Iris Marion, ed. *The Thinking Muse: Feminism and Modern French Philosophy*. Bloomington: Indiana University Press, 1989.

Anderson, Mark. "Anorexia and Modernism, or How I Learned to Diet in All Directions." *Discourse* 11.1 (Fall–Winter 1988–89):28–41.

Anzaldua, Gloria and Morgan, Cherrie, ed. *This Bridge Called My Back: Writings by Radical Women of Color*. Watertown, MA: Persephone Press, 1981.

Arendt, Hannah. *Between Past and Future*. New York: Penguin, 1954.

———. *Imperialism*. New York: Harcourt Brace Jovanovich, 1951.

———. *Lectures in Kant's Political Philosophy*, edited by Ronald Beiner. Chicago: The University of Chicago Press, 1982.

———. *On Revolution*. New York: The Viking Press, 1963.

———. *The Human Condition*. Chicago: University of Chicago Press, 1958.

Baynes, Kenneth, Bohman, James, and McCarthy, Thomas, ed. *After Philosophy: End or Transformation?* Cambridge, MA: The MIT Press, 1987.

Bauman, Zygmut. "Is There A Postmodern Society?" *Theory Culture Society* 5:217–27.

Benhabib, Seyla. *Critique, Norm and Utopia*. New York: Columbia University Press, 1986.

Bennington, Geoff, "August: Double Justice." *Diacritics* 3 (Fall 1984):64–43.

Bordo, Susan, and Jagger, Alison, ed. *Gender/Body/Knowledge: Feminist Reconstruction of Being and Knowing*. New Brunswick, NJ: Rutgers University Press, 1989.

Bourdieu, Pierre. *Distinction: A Social Critique of the Judgement of Taste*, translated by Richard Nice. Cambridge, MA: Harvard University Press, 1984.

Butler, Judith. "Variations on Sex and Gender: Beauvoir, Wittig, and Foucault." *Praxis International*. 5(4 January 1986): 505–16.

———. *Subjects of Desire: Hegelian Reflections in Twentieth-Century France*. New York: Columbia University Press, 1987.

149

Carroll David. "Rephrasing the Political with Kant and Lyotard: From Aesthetic to Political Judgement." *Diacritics* 3 (Fall 1984):74–89.

——. *The Subject in Question: Languages and the Strategies of Fiction.* Chicago: The University of Chicago Press, 1982.

Cixous, Hélène, and Clement, Catherine. *The Newly Born Woman*, translated by Betsy Wing. Minneapolis: The University of Minnesota Press, 1986.

Culler, Jonathan. *Framing the Sign: Criticism and Its Institutions.* Norman, OK: University of Oklahoma Press, 1988.

——. *The Pursuit of Signs: Semiotics, Literature, Deconstruction.* Ithaca, NY: Cornell University Press, 1981.

Deleuze, Gilles and Guattari, Felix. *Anti-Oedipus*, edited by Robert Hurley, Mark Seem, and Helen R. Lane. Minneapolis: The University of Minnesota Press, 1983.

——. *A Thousand Plateaus: Capitalism And Schizophrenia*, translated by Brian Massume. Minneapolis: The University of Minnesota Press, 1987.

Deleuze, Gilles and Parnet, Claire. *Dialogues*, translated by Hugh Tomlinson and Barbara Habberjam. New York: Columbia University Press, 1987.

Derrida, Jacques. *Of Gramatology.* Baltimore: Johns Hopkins U Press, 1976.

——. *Writing and Difference.* Chicago: Chicago U Press, 1978.

Dews, Peter, "The Letter and the Discourse and its Other in Lyotard." *Diacritics* 3 (Fall 1984):40–51.

Diamond, Irene, and Quinby, Lee ed. *Feminism and Foucault: Reflection on Resistance.* Boston: Northeastern University Press, 1988.

Dreyfus, Hubert L., and Paul Rabinow. *Michel Foucault: Beyond Structuralism and Hermeneutics.* 2nd. edition. With an Afterward and Interview with Michel Foucault. Chicago: University of Chicago Press, 1983.

Ecker, Gisela. *Feminist Aesthetics*, translated by Harriet Anderson. Boston: Beacon Press, 1985.

Export, Valie. "The Real and Its Double: The Body." *Discourse* 11.1 (Fall–Winter 1988–89):3–27.

Foucault, Michel. "A Conversation with Michel Foucault." *Christopher Street*, no.64 (May 1982): 36–41.

——. *The Birth of the Clinic: An Archaeology of Medical Perception*, translated by A.M. Sheridan Smith. New York: Vintage/Random House, 1975.

——. *Discipline and Punish: The Birth of the Prison*, translated by Alan Sheridan. New York: Vintage/Random House, 1979.

——. "Final Interview; Michel Foucault." *Raritan Review* 5 (Summer 1985): 1–13.

——. *Herculine Barbin: Being the Recently Discovered Memoirs of a Nineteenth Century French Hermaphrodite*, translated by Richard McDougall. New York: Pantheon, 1980.

——. *The History of Sexuality, Volume I: An Introduction*, translated by Robert Hurley. New York: Vintage/Random House, 1980.

——. *Language. Counter-Memory, Practice: Selected Essays and Interviews*, edited by Donald F. Bouchard. Ithaca, NY: Cornell University Press, 1977.

———. *Madness and Civilization: A History of Insanity in the Age of Reason*, translated by R. Howard. New York: Vintage/Random House, 1973.

———. *Power/Knowledge: Selected Interviews and Other Writings*. New York: Random House, 1981.

———. "Power and Sex: An Interview." *Telos* 32 (summer 1977):152–61.

———. "Politics and the Study of Discourse." *Ideology and Consciousness* 3 (1978):7–26.

———. *The Use of Pleasure Volume 2 of the History of Sexuality*, translated by Robert Hurley. New York: Pantheon, 1985.

Fraser, Nancy. "Foucault's Body-Languages: A Post-Humanist Political Rhetoric?" *Salmagundi* 61 (Fall 1983): 50–70.

———. "Foucault on Modern Power: Empirical Insights and Normative Confusions." *Praxis International* 1 (October 1981): 272–87.

———. "Michel Foucault: A 'Young Conservative'?" *Ethics* 96 (October 1985): 165–84.

———. "Toward a Discourse Ethic of Solidarity." *Praxis International* 5:425–29.

———. *Unruly Practices: Power, Discourse and Gender in Contemporary Social Theory*. Minneapolis: The University of Minnesota Press, 1889.

Gamma, Loraine, and Marshment, Margaret, ed. *The Female Gaze: Women as Viewers of Popular Culture*. Seattle, WA: The Real Comet Press, 1989.

Habermas, Jürgen. *The Philosophical Discourse of Modernity: Twelve Lectures*, translated by Fredrick Lawrence. Cambridge, MA: The MIT Press, 1987.

Heller, Agnes. "The Dissatisfied Society." *Praxis International* 2 (1983):359–70.

———. "Individual and Community." *Social Practice* 1 (1983):11–22.

———. "The Moral Situation in Modernity," presented at Temple University, Fall 1987.

Heller, Thomas, and Wellbery, David. *Reconstructing Individualism: Autonomy, Individuality, and the Self in Western Thought*. Stanford: Stanford University Press, 1986.

Hicks, Laurie. "A Feminist Analysis of Empowerment and Community in Art Education," *Studies in Art Education* Vol. 32, no. 1 (Fall 1990): 36–46.

hooks, bell. *Yearning: Race, Gender, and Cultural Politics*. Boston, MA: South End Press, 1990.

Hoy, David Couzins, ed. *Foucault, a Critical Reader*. Oxford: Basil Blackwell, 1986.

Jameson, Fredric. *The Prison House of Language*. Princeton: Princeton University Press, 1972.

Kellner, Douglas. "Postmodernism as Social Theory: Some Challenges and Problems." *Theory Culture and Society* 5 (1988):239–69.

King, Richard. "Self-Realization and Solidarity: Rorty and the Judging Self," in *Pragmatism's Freud: The Moral Disposition of Psychoanalysis*, edited by William Kerrigan and Joseph H. Smith. Baltimore: The Johns Hopkins University Press, 1986.

Lacan, Jacques. *Ecrítes. A Selection*. London: Tavistock, 1977.

Laclau, Ernesto, and Chantal Mouffe. *Hegemony and Socialist Strategy: Toward a Radical Democratic Politics.*, translated by Winston Moore and Paul Cammack. Norfolk: The Thetford Press Ltd., 1985.

Lorde, Audre. *Sister Outsider*. Trumansburg, NY: Crossing Press, 1984.

Lotringer, Sylvere, ed. *Foucault Live: Interviews, 1966–84*. New York: Semiotext(e) Foreign Agents Series, 1989.

Lyotard, Jean-Francois. *The Differend: Phrases in Dispute*, translated by Georges Van Den Abbeele. Minneapolis: The University of Minnesota Press, 1988.

———. "The Differend, The Referent, And the Proper Name." *Diacritics* 3 (Fall 1984): 4–15.

———. "Interview" with Georges Van Den Abbeele, in *Diacritics* 3 (Fall 1984):16–24.

———. *Just Gaming*, translated by Wlad Godzich. Minneapolis: The University of Minnesota Press, 1985.

———. *The Postmodern Condition: A Report on Knowledge*, translated by Geoff Bennington and Brian Massumi. Minneapolis: The University of Minnesota Press, 1984.

Macpherson, C.B. London: Oxford University Press, 1962.

Margolis, Joseph. *Pragmatism Without Foundations: Reconciling Realism and Relativism*. Oxford: Basil Blackwell, 1986.

———. "Reinterpreting Interpretation." *Journal of Aesthetics*. 1988.

———. "Redeeming Foucault," forthcoming in a collection to be put together by John D. Caputo and Mark Yount.

Maslan, Mark. "Foucault and Pragmatism." *Raritan* 7 (Winter 1988):94–114.

Miller, James. *The Passion of Foucault*. New York: Simon and Schuster, 1993.

Mitchell, W.J.T., ed. *The Politics of Interpretation*. Chicago: The University of Chicago Press, 1982.

Moi, Toni, ed. *French Feminist Thought: A Reader*. Oxford: Basil Blackwell, 1987.

Morrison, Toni. *The Bluest Eye*. New York: Washington Square Press, 1970.

Nehamas, Alexander. *Nietzsche: Life as Literature*. Cambridge, MA: Harvard University Press, 1985.

Nicholson, Linda, J., ed. *Feminism/Postmodernism*. New York: Routledge, 1990.

Nochlin, Linda. *Women, Art, and Power and Other Essays*. New York: Harper and Row, 1988.

Oakshott, Michel. *On Human Conduct*. Oxford: Clarendon Press, 1975.

Pettit, Philip. *The Concept of Structuralism A Critical Analysis*. Berkeley: University of California Press, 1977.

Pollock, Griselda. *Vision and Difference: Femininity, Feminism, and the Histories of Art*. London: Routledge, 1988.

Rorty, Richard. *The Consequences of Pragmatism*. Minneapolis: University of Minnesota Press, 1982.

———. *Contingency Irony, and Solidarity*. Cambridge: Cambridge University Press, 1989.

———. "Freud and Moral Reflection." William Kerrigan and J.H. Smith eds. Baltimore: The Johns Hopkins University Press, 1986.

———. "Freud, Morality and Hermeneutics." *New Literary History* 12.

———. "Habermas and Lyotard on Postmodernity." *Praxis International* 4:32–44.

———. "Postmodernist Bourgeois Liberalism." *Journal of Philosophy* 80:583–89.

——. "Priority of Democracy to Philosophy." *Virginia Statute for Religious Freedom*, Merrill D. Peterson and Robert C. Vaughan ed. Cambridge: Cambridge University Press, 1988.

Ross, Andrew. *Universal Abandon? The Politics of Postmodernism*. Minneapolis: The University of Minnesota Press,1988.

Sandel, Michel ed. *Liberalism and its Critics*. New York: New York University Press, 1984.

Sandel, Michel. *Liberalism and the Limits of Justice*, Cambridge: Cambridge University Press, 1982.

Saussure, Ferdinand de. *Course in General Linguistics*, translated by Wade Baskin. New York: McGraw-Hill Book Company, 1966.

Sawicki, Jana. "Foucault and Feminism: Toward a Politics of Difference." *Hypatia* 1, no.2. (Fall 1986): 1–13.

——. "On Using Foucault for Feminism: A Personal Reflection," presented at the Eastern Division of the American Philosophical Association SWIPP meeting, December 1989, Atlanta, Georgia.

——. "The Politics of Difference: Towards a Radical Pluralism," presented at the Third International Social Philosophy Conference, Charlotte, North Carolina, June, 1987.

Schoenfielder, Lisa and Wieser, Barb, ed. *Shadow on a Tightrope: Writings by Women on Fat Oppression*. San Francisco: Spinsters/Aunt Lute Book Company, 1983.

Shusterman, Richard. "Convention, Variations on a Theme." *Philosophical Investigations* 9(1986).

——. "Postmodern Aestheticism: A New Moral Philosophy?" *Theory Culture and Society* 5: 335–355.

——. "Postmodernism and the Aesthetic Turn." *Poetics Today*, 9:1989.

——. "Saving Art from Aesthetics." *Poetics Today* 9 (1988).

Tinder, Glenn. *Community: Reflections on a Tragic Ideal*. Baton Rouge: Louisiana State University Press, 1980.

Smith, Paul. *Discerning the Subject*. Minneapolis: The University of Minnesota Press, 1988.

Walzer, Michael. *Obligations: Essays in Disobedience, War and Citizenship*. Cambridge, MA: Harvard University Press, 1982.

——. "Political Action: The Problems of Dirty Hands." *Philosophy and Public Affairs* 2:160–81.

——. *Spheres of Justice: A Defense of Pluralism and Equality*. New York: Basic Books, 1983.

Weedon, Chris. *Feminist Practices and Poststructuralist Theory*. Oxford: Basil Blackwell, 1987.

West, Cornel. *Race Matters*. Boston: Beacon Press, 1993.

Wittgenstein, Ludwig. *Philosophical Investigations*. New York: Macmillan Publishing Co., Inc., 1953.

Young, Iris Marion. "The Ideal of Community and the Politics of Difference." *Social Theory and Practice*. 12 (1986):1–26.

Index